RATIONAL EXPECTATIONS

CAMBRIDGE SURVEYS OF ECONOMIC LITERATURE

Editors:
Professor Phyllis Deane, University of Cambridge, and
Professor Mark Perlman, University of Pittsburgh

Editorial Advisory Board:
Professor A. B. Atkinson, London School of Economics and Political Science
Professor M. Bronfenbrenner, Duke University
Professor K. D. George, University College, Cardiff
Professor C. P. Kindleberger, Massachusetts Institute of Technology
Professor T. Mayer, University of California, Davis
Professor A. R. Prest, London School of Economics and Political Science

The literature of economics is expanding rapidly, and many subjects have changed out of recognition within the space of a few years. Perceiving the state of knowledge in fast-developing subjects is difficult for students and time-consuming for professional economists. This series of books is intended to help with this problem. Each book will be quite brief, giving a clear structure to and balanced overview of the topic, and written at a level intelligible to the senior undergraduate. They will therefore be useful for teaching but will also provide a mature yet compact presentation of the subject for economists wishing to update their knowledge outside their own specialism.

Other books in the series
E. Roy Weintraub: Microfoundations: The compatibility of microeconomics and macroeconomics
Dennis C. Mueller: Public choice
Robert Clark and Joseph Spengler: The economics of individual and population aging
Edwin Burmeister: Capital theory and dynamics
Mark Blaug: The methodology of economics or how economists explain
Robert Ferber and Werner Z. Hirsch: Social experimentation and economic policy
Anthony C. Fisher: Resource and environmental economics
Morton I. Kamien and Nancy L. Schwartz: Market structure and innovation
Richard E. Caves: Multinational enterprise and economic analysis
Mark R. Killingsworth: Labor supply
Anne O. Krueger: Exchange-rate determination

Rational expectations

STEVEN M. SHEFFRIN

Department of Economics
University of California, Davis

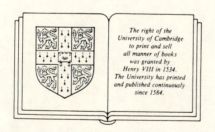

The right of the
University of Cambridge
to print and sell
all manner of books
was granted by
Henry VIII in 1534.
The University has printed
and published continuously
since 1584.

CAMBRIDGE UNIVERSITY PRESS

CAMBRIDGE

LONDON   NEW YORK   NEW ROCHELLE

MELBOURNE   SYDNEY

Published by the Press Syndicate of the University of Cambridge
The Pitt Building, Trumpington Street, Cambridge CB2 1RP
32 East 57th Street, New York, NY 10022, USA
296 Beaconsfield Parade, Middle Park, Melbourne 3206, Australia

First published 1983
Reprinted 1983, 1984, 1985

Printed in the United States of America

Library of Congress Cataloging in Publication Data

Sheffrin, Steven M.
Rational expectations.
(Cambridge surveys of economic literature)
Bibliography: p.
Includes index.
1. Rational expectation (Economic theory)
2. Macroeconomics.   I. Title.   II. Series.
HB172.5.S523   1983   339   82–19747
ISBN 0 521 24310 6   hard covers
ISBN 0 521 28595 X   paperback

To my parents

CONTENTS

PREFACE

More than most areas in economics, macroeconomics has been in a state of flux during the past decade, partly because of the rather poor performance of the economy, which naturally created a spirit of unrest. Perhaps of more importance was the academic quest to redevelop the foundations of macroeconomics that occupied the time of so many scholars. The development of the body of thought associated with the term "rational expectations" was an outcome of this effort.

Despite the impact that rational expectations has had in the development of macroeconomic theory, to most economists it still appears to be an extreme and controversial set of ideas with only little "policy relevance." Indeed, a substantial number (a majority?) of macroeconomists also share this position.

This book takes the opposite point of view. Its basic thesis is that the work on rational expectations has not only been important for understanding macroeconomics and financial markets but has fundamental and striking implications for other areas as well. This does not mean that, at present, there is a substantive consensus in macroeconomics – there is not. But the process of rethinking macroeconomic theory has had a pronounced influence on the methods and questions in the field, which, in turn, will influence economic inquiry in other areas.

As a survey of the subject, this book attempts to take a balanced view of the work associated with rational expectations. It begins, in the first chapter, with a broad discussion of the concept and the a priori case for the use of rational expectations in economic analysis. Subsequent chapters explore the contributions of work related to rational expectations in macroeconomics, financial market theory, and areas of microeconomics. Throughout, existing empirical evidence is integrated with the theoretical discussions. The final chapter gives a broad overview of what has and has not been accomplished.

The technical demands on the reader have been kept to a minimum, with the relatively simple mathematical ideas developed where needed in the discussion. The cost of this decision is that many of the important econometric issues can only be described in general terms. However, the survey should provide the necessary orientation to guide the reader to more advanced material.

I first started to study macroeconomics at the time when the Phillips curve began to shift and the common explanation for this shift was the change in inflationary expectations. I recall my mood of pessimism about the future of the discipline of economics when it appeared that psychological phenomena were so central to the subject. Rational expectations is an answer, although not a full antidote, to this pessimism.

It would be impossible to acknowledge all the conversations that influenced the course of this book. Several individuals made especially important contributions to this project: Jim Barth, Bob Driskill, Tom Mayer, and Rick Mishkin all read the entire manuscript and provided insightful comments; Colin Day, the editor for the project, guided me nicely along to completion; and both Anne Jones and Ginny Purdum typed and retyped the manuscript. Finally, I am extremely grateful to my wife Anjali for her sustained interest in this work and her overall support.

S. M. S.

1

The concept of rational expectations

Two divergent schools of thought originated at Carnegie-Mellon University in the late 1950s and early 1960s. During this period Herbert A. Simon had been refining his ideas on "bounded" rationality, a doctrine stressing man's* limited computational abilities in making decisions. At the same time, his colleague, John F. Muth, was working in another direction and developing the doctrine of rational expectations. Adding intrigue to this episode was the fact that Simon and Muth (along with Franco Modigliani and Charles Holt) were also collaborating on a book on inventory management and production control. Although the development of the diverse doctrines of bounded rationality and rational expectations by collaborators could be viewed as just an historical coincidence, it is more likely that an intense preoccupation with a common set of problems led the two researchers on different paths in search of a solution.

In their joint effort Simon and Muth worked on problems of production scheduling and inventory management for the firm. These problems had been studied by many talented mathematicians, economists, and operations researchers who had developed general results for complex cases. The work of Holt, Modigliani, Muth, and Simon (1960) was aimed at deriving tractable, operational rules that could

---

* To avoid awkward wording, "man" and the pronoun "he" will sometimes be used generically, referring to both sexes.

be easily applied in practice. As simplifying devices, they assumed that the various costs facing a company could be described by linear or quadratic cost functions. Why was this a useful simplification?

Simon (1956) had earlier shown that with quadratic costs and certain assumptions about the nature of uncertainty in the model, rules describing the optimal behavior for production and inventories for the firm would be linear functions of observable variables. In addition, in this framework, firms need only to consider the *expected value* of future sales and could ignore other moments of the probability distribution of sales. This result, known as *certainty equivalence*, makes the calculation of inventory policies much easier by reducing the computational load for a typical decision maker.

Simon (1979) viewed the simplifications needed to obtain the certainty equivalence result in a positive light. He wrote, "the assumption of quadratic costs reduces the original problem to one that is readily solved. Of course, the solution, though it provides optimal decisions for the simplified world of our assumptions, provides, at best, satisfactory solutions for the real-world decision problem that the quadratic function approximates. In principle, unattainable optimization is sacrificed for in-practice, attainable satisfaction" (1979:499).

This approach, obtaining optimal solutions for a simplified world, is one strategy for easing the computational burden on decision makers. Another route is to give up explicit optimization and search for satisfactory solutions for a more realistic world. In Simon's terminology, both these strategies are examples of *satisficing* behavior, behavior that eschews complete optimization in favor of a more limited search for the best policy or decision.

Simon, therefore, viewed the certainty-equivalence results as a useful approximation for certain situations but did not elevate them to the plateau of a foundation for a general theory of economic behavior. In other environments different types of satisficing behavior might be more appropriate. In some situations the decision maker has to search out further alternatives rather than choose among given alternatives. Because decision makers must decide when to choose, an extra level of complexity to problem solving is added.

Certainty-equivalence, therefore, was a useful, but by no means all-encompassing, paradigm for behavior.

John Muth viewed the problem somewhat differently. The certainty-equivalence results, which enabled the investigator to focus only on the *expected values* of variables that were uncertain, provided the key to an attack on another problem, which could loosely be termed the "interaction between expectations and reality." There were many examples of this problem in the literature at the time – perhaps the most well known concerned the "cobweb theorem" in agriculture.

The work of Nerlove (1958) and others stressed that farmers' planting decisions depended on the prices they expected to receive when the crop was marketed. In turn, the actual price for the crop depended on the amount finally harvested and the current level of demand. It was soon evident that different assumptions concerning the formation of price expectations could radically alter the actual price dynamics in the market. For example, if farmers based their price expectations on last year's price, there was a potential for dramatic instability in prices and production. Suppose that a spell of bad weather one year destroys part of the crop so that prices rise above normal. If farmers expect this high price to prevail, they will plant more than usual and when the resulting crop is harvested, prices will fall below normal. If this low price, in turn, is expected to persist, plantings will be lower than usual, leading to less output and higher prices. Depending on the parameters of demand and supply curves, these price oscillations could either grow over time or dampen. Other price expectation schemes would lead to different dynamic behavior for prices and production.

Another example of this phenomenon that was prominent in the literature of the 1950s concerned the dynamics of hyperinflation. Cagan (1956) developed a simple model in which the velocity of money depended inversely on expected inflation, whereas expected inflation, in turn, was a function of past inflation. His model had the property that an autonomous increase in expected inflation would lead to an increase in velocity, which, in turn, would cause prices to rise. The increase in prices would then increase expectations of inflation, leading to a further increase in velocity. Depending on key parameters in the model, the burst of inflation caused by an autonomous change in expectations could either dampen or accelerate into a hyperinflation.

In both cases the explicit dynamics for prices depended on the precise nature of price expectations. Subsequent research demonstrated that these models were not robust to changes in the way expectations were formed, and theoretical and empirical work rested critically on the exact specification of the price expectation mechanisms.

Progress in economics, therefore, seemed to require a working, quantitative knowledge of how expectations of key variables were formed. Unfortunately, this verified theory of expectation formation existed neither at the time nor today. If anything, the psychological literature on expectations tends to suggest that people's expectations are intimately connected to their particular situation, and no general theory seems to work. Tversky and Kahneman (1974) presented evidence that decision makers are often subject to certain biases that naturally arise out of their circumstances. For example, they argued that individuals, as a rule, judge distances by the clarity of objects in their field of vision. If objects are sharply perceived, then they are judged to be close at hand. This works well in most circumstances but, at times, can give very misleading results. Distances will be overestimated when visibility is poor because objects will then be seen with less clarity. On the other hand, when visibility is exceptionally good, distances will be underestimated. Although these insights may be useful to predict behavior in certain situations, they are unlikely to become the foundation of a theory of aggregate behavior.

With the behavior of models so sensitive to the formulation of expectations, the lack of a general theory of expectations was an unsatisfactory state of affairs. It would be ludicrous for policy advice to be made contingent on what economists think the public believes.

In his path-breaking article, "Rational Expectations and the Theory of Price Movements," John Muth (1961:315) recognized this problem. "To make dynamic economic models complete, various expectational formulas have been used. There is, however, little evidence to suggest that the presumed relations bear a resemblance to the way the economy works." Muth suggested that economists are often interested in how expectations might change in certain circumstances and thus should not be satisfied with fixed expectational formulas that do not allow for change when, for example, the structure of the system changes. If the underlying economic system changes, we would expect economic actors, at least after a certain amount of time, to change the way they form their expectations. Traditional models of expectation formation do not permit this adaptation.

In a modest manner, Muth (1961:316) put forward his hypothesis: "I should like to suggest that expectations, since they are informed predictions of future events, are essentially the same as the predictions of the relevant economic theory. At the risk of confusing this purely descriptive hypothesis with a pronouncement as to what firms ought to do, we call such expectations 'rational.' "

Muth noted that many economists, including Simon, thought that theories based on rational behavior were inadequate to explain observed phenomena. Muth argued the exact opposite point: Existing economic models did not assume enough rational behavior. One way to ensure this rationality was to insist that expectations of economic actors be consistent with the models used to explain their behavior. Muth's insight was that it was possible to require economic agents to form expectations of economic variables by using the very model that actually determined these variables. This ensured that the behavior of the model was consistent with individual actors' beliefs about the behavior of the economic system. Although this was Muth's basic point, a more formal and precise definition of rational expectations requires a review of several concepts from the theory of probability.

Conditional expectations and Muthian rationality

To understand the logic of rational expectations, one must be familiar with the concepts of probability densities, conditional probability densities, and the expectation operator. Although most of the economic examples use continuous random variables, for expositional purposes, it is useful to begin with discrete random variables. Let X be a random variable (such as a grade on a final exam) that can take on any of the values $X_1, \ldots, X_n$.

Let P_i be the probability that the random variable actually takes on the value X_i. The vector of probabilities $P_1 \ldots, P_n$ completely describes the information about the stochastic behavior of the random variable.

The expected value of a discrete random variable is the traditional measure of the central tendency of a probability distribution. It is defined as

$$\text{expected value} = E(X) = \sum_{i=1}^{n} P_i \cdot X_i \qquad (1.1)$$

For continuous random variables there are similar definitions. A continuous random variable can take on any value within a certain specified interval; for example, the amount of rainfall on a given day can be described as a continuous random variable ranging between zero and a positive number that reflects the heaven's rainfall capacity. A density function $f(X)$ describes the probability of various levels of rainfall. More precisely, $f(X) \, dX$ is the probability that the rainfall will be in the small interval dX around the level X. For continuous random variables the expected value is defined as

$$\text{expected value} = E(X) = \int_a^b Xf(X) \, dX \qquad (1.2)$$

where a and b are the lower and upper limits, respectively, of the random variable.

Conditional probability or conditional density functions are used extensively in the rational expectations literature. To understand this concept, imagine that a stranger approaches you on a train and wants to play a game of chance with a die that he removes from his pocket. You inspect the die, notice that it has six numbers and no obvious deformities. In your own mind you assign a probability of one-sixth to an occurrence of each number on the die.

Suppose, however, that an hour before the stranger approached you, a conductor on the train had wandered up and down the aisles warning the passengers about a stranger with a loaded die. In particular, the conductor told you the die came up on the number three half the time while the other numbers split the remaining probability. Warned with this information, you would now assign 50 percent probability to the occurrence of a 3 and 10 percent probability to the occurrence of each of the other numbers.

There are now two different probability distributions – one corresponds to the case in which you were warned and the other to the situation in which you were at the mercy of the stranger with the loaded die. In the former case your probability distribution can be described as *conditional* on being warned by the conductor. This is a simple example of the concept of a conditional probability distribution.

More generally, economic actors will make their probability assessments based on the information available to them at the time. Let I_{t-1} signify the information set that is available to economic actors at time $t - 1$. Then the notation $f(X_t|I_{t-1})$ will stand for the *conditional probability* density for the random variable X_t, given the information available at time $t - 1$.

Corresponding to the conditional density is the *conditional expectation* defined as

$$\left.\begin{array}{l}\text{conditional}\\\text{expectation}\end{array}\right\} = E[X_t|I_{t-1}] = \int_a^b X_t f(X_t|I_{t-1})\, dX_t \quad (1.3)$$

The conditional expectation of a random variable is just the expected value of the variable formed by using the conditional density.

To understand some properties of conditional expectations, one should think of conditional expectations as forecasts of random variables. Associated with any forecast is a forecast error, ϵ_t, defined as

$$\text{forecast error} = \epsilon_t = X_t - E[X_t|I_{t-1}] \quad (1.4)$$

The forecast error has two important properties. First, the conditional expectation of the forecast error is zero. This follows directly from noting that, at time $t - 1$, the conditional expectation (or the forecast) is known so that its conditional expectation is just the forecast itself. Using this fact, one finds that the conditional expectation of the forecast error is

$$E[\epsilon_t | I_{t-1}] = E[X_t | I_{t-1}] - E[X_t | I_{t-1}] = 0 \qquad (1.5)$$

The second property of the forecast errors is known as the *orthogonality property*. Forecast errors should not only have a zero expected value but should also be uncorrelated with any information that is available to economic actors. If this were not the case it would be possible to improve the forecast by incorporating this correlation into the forecast. To put it simply, an indication of a good forecast (and a property of conditional expectations) is that any subsequent forecast errors should be inherently unpredictable and hence unrelated to any information available at the time the forecast is formulated. Symbolically, the orthogonality principle can be expressed as

$$E[\epsilon_t \cdot I_{t-1} | I_{t-1}] = 0 \qquad (1.6)$$

Forecast errors derived from conditional expectations are uncorrelated with any information that is contained in the available information set. Shiller (1978) provides a further discussion of this important property.

Muth's rational expectations hypothesis essentially equates two distinct concepts; economic actors' subjective, psychological expectations of economic variables are postulated to be the mathematical conditional expectation of those variables. Or, in other words, people's subjective expectations are, on average, equal to the true values of the variable.

This idea can be clarified by some notation. Let $_{t-1}X_t^\epsilon$ be the subjective, psychological expectation for a variable X_t. Drawing on the previous notation, Muth's hypothesis asserts that

$$\left.\begin{array}{l}\text{subjective}\\ \text{expectation}\end{array}\right\} = \,_{t-1}X_t^\epsilon = E[X_t | I_{t-1}] = \left\{\begin{array}{l}\text{conditional}\\ \text{expectation}\end{array}\right. \qquad (1.7)$$

Thus there is a connection between the beliefs of individual economic actors and the actual stochastic behavior of the system. This is the essence of the rational expectations approach.

To understand the implications of Muth's concept, one should distinguish between the problem of forecasting variables that are exogenous to the system and those that are endogenous to the system. For variables that are exogenous to the system, forecasts or expectations by economic agents are important but do not affect the actual values of the exogenous variables. Exogenous variables are, by definition, those that are determined *outside* the existing system. On the other hand, expectations or forecasts of endogenous variables will affect the dynamics of the endogenous variables. The example of the farmers illustrates this point – their expectations about prices (an endogenous variable) affect the behavior of the endogenous variables (prices and quantities).

The hypothesis of rational expectations applies to both exogenous and endogenous variables but is most interesting for endogenous variables. Expectations are rational if, given the economic model, they will produce actual values of variables that will, on average, equal the expectations. Expectations will diverge from actual values only because of some unpredictable uncertainty in the system. If there were no unpredictable uncertainty, expectations of variables would coincide with the actual values – there would be *perfect foresight*. The rational expectations hypothesis differs from perfect foresight because it allows for uncertainty in economic systems.

The example with the farmers should help to clarify the concept. A farmer with rational expectations performs the following thought experiment: What price can I expect so that if everyone else anticipates the same price, on average, we will all be correct? The farmer takes into account the anticipated supplies from his decisions, the decisions of similarly situated farmers, and calculates the price that will prevail if they all expect a particular price. In other words, they behave as if they possess a competitive, stochastic model of the market.

Farmers need not, of course, actually perform this thought experiment; as Milton Friedman has stressed, economic actors need only act *as if* they are maximizing utility or profits for our theories to work. Muth (1961:317) was quite explicit on this point: "[the hypothesis] . . . *does not* assert that the scratch work of entrepreneurs resembles the system of equations in any way."

It is not necessary for individuals to have identical expectations for economists to use the rational expectations hypothesis. Muth argued that individuals' expectations should, however, be distributed around the true expected value of the variable to be forecasted. In this way the average of individual forecasts would be the expected value of the true variable although individuals could certainly differ in their beliefs.

Once the fiction of identical individuals is abandoned, it is possible to take another perspective on the rational expectations hypothesis and consider it from the point of view of arbitrage. In ordinary markets we do not require that all individuals respond to price signals in order to maintain a vibrant price system. Instead, we recognize that only a handful of individuals is required to arbitrage markets and ensure that, for example, coffee sells at the same transportation-cost-adjusted price in all locations. The same principle applies to the rational expectations hypothesis. If there is any economic profit to be gained from gathering and analyzing information in order to predict the future, we would expect some individuals to pursue this strategy. If enough arbitrage activity takes place, the market may behave as if it is rational even though many individuals in the market are simply passive.

The arbitrage perspective leads quickly to two points: (1) It suggests that the rational expectations hypothesis may be especially applicable to markets (such as financial markets) in which arbitrage is relatively costless. (2) It suggests that survey evidence that measures *average* rather than *marginal* beliefs or behavior may provide a misleading perspective on the applicability of the rational expectations hypothesis. The rational expectations hypothesis is not synonymous with arbitrage – it is certainly possible for a market to behave in a manner consistent with the rational expectations hypothesis even when arbitrage activities are costly. When arbitrage activity is relatively costless, however, this perspective provides an additional rationale for the use of the hypothesis.

The certainty-equivalence proposition was used extensively in Muth's article. Muth made the necessary assumptions to ensure that rational economic agents, for the most part, need only concern themselves with the mean or expected value of future variables and not worry about higher moments of the probability distribution such as the variance. Muth, of course, recognized this as a simplification and thought that it was simply the price for obtaining some interesting and meaningful results. Subsequent work in the 1970s [e.g., Lucas (1978a)] illustrated that it was possible to build models in which people's entire subjective probability distribution would coincide with the true objective probability distributions governing the system. This is the most general statement of the rational expectations hypothesis: The subjective probability distributions of economic actors equal the objective probability distributions in the system.

It is clear from the structure of Muth's (1961) article – theoretical analysis followed by some empirical applications – that he viewed the rational expectations hypothesis as a hypothesis of *positive* economics. The hypothesis could be wrong – it might be the case that expectation schemes did not have any consistent properties across economic models. If they did, however, powerful analytical results might be possible. In the sense that Muth was just proposing a hypothesis, his work may strike some as less dogmatic than Simon's. Simon's contention that expectations cannot embody too much rationality is as testable as Muth's conjecture that they may be more rational than commonly believed. Before putting the shackles on individual's expectations and condemning them to a world of limitations and bounds, it may be useful, Muth argued, for economic science to explore precisely the opposite alternative.

A priori critiques of Muthian rationality

Much of the criticism and hostility toward Muth's concept of rationality that surfaces in some quarters can be traced to two factors. Sometimes the hypothesis has been employed in models that are thought to be simplistic. This, however, is not a criticism of the rational expectations hypothesis per se as much as it is a dissatisfaction with certain types of model building. On the other hand, some writers have rebelled at the idea that Muth's definition is the best, or even an adequate, definition of true rational behavior.

The rational expectations hypothesis has been criticized for being, among other things, inconsistent with the subjectivist view of probability; an inadequate description of procedural rationality; and not a sufficiently general hypothesis to include learning and adaptive behavior.

The subjectivist critique of the rational expectations hypothesis, as outlined in Swamy, Barth, and Tinsley (1982), focuses on the central role that objective probability distributions play in the theory. Subjectivists recoil at the notion of a true or objective probability distribution apart from the beliefs of particular agents. From the subjectivist point of view, probability beliefs are essentially the "bets" that an individual would be willing to make about the occurrence of a set of events. As Savage (1954) has shown, an internally consistent subjective probability measure can be derived for the individual if his choices among hypothetical bets satisfy certain axioms. Although different individuals may be willing to make different bets, as long as the bets of each individual satisfy the axioms, each individual can be said to be behaving in a consistent, coherent, and even "rational" manner. There is no need for individual probability beliefs to coincide with either each other or some outside "objective" standard. Thus the subjectivists would argue that there already exists a standard for rational behavior that bears little resemblance to the rational expectations hypothesis.

Robert E. Lucas, who engineered the rational expectations "revolution" in macroeconomics, has defended the rational expectations hypothesis from the subjectivist attack. Lucas did not dispute the subjectivist or Bayesian theory of the foundation of probability. However, he argued that

> the general hypothesis that economic agents are Bayesian
> decision makers has, in many applications, little
> empirical content: without some way of inferring what
> an agent's subjective view of the future is, this
> hypothesis is of no help in understanding his behavior.
> Even psychotic behavior can be (and today, is)
> understood as "rational" given a sufficiently abnormal
> view of relevant probabilities. (1977:15)

To employ economic theory in practice, Lucas argues, one must know what probability distributions agents actually use.

In situations in which it is possible to observe the frequencies of different events, it may make sense to assume that agents' subjective probability distributions mirror the observed frequencies. Lucas concedes that there may be situations where observed frequencies provide little guide to decision makers. In these circumstances Lucas argues that *no* economic reasoning will be of any value. In short, economic science requires some theory about the content of subjective probability beliefs; when it is possible, observed frequencies may be a useful guide to these beliefs. Predictive theories cannot be easily built on the principle that agents have subjective probability distributions that cannot be related to objective events.

One of the implications of Muth's definition of rational expectations is that agents' expectations about variables should change when the conditional probability distribution governing the variables changes. This aspect of the theory has been challenged by Peter Rappoport (1980) on the grounds that it is inconsistent with a broader definition of rationality.

Rappoport takes as his paradigm for rationality the textbook story about the logic of scientific inference. According to this view, existing hypotheses are maintained until some evidence dictates that the hypothesis be rejected. In this spirit Rappoport argues for a reliance on classical hypothesis testing to determine if a particular expectation mechanism is no longer consistent with the data. Because this theory is consistent with the logic of scientific progress, Rappoport argues that it deserves consideration as the primary theory of expectation formation.

This version of procedural rationality may, indeed, be an interesting theory of expectation formation but it gains little independent support from its connection to the well-known falsification methodology of modern science. There are two grounds for skepticism. First, today it is generally believed that philosophy oversteps its bounds when it recommends substantive theories for a science; at best, philosophy is useful for clearing conceptual puzzles that may arise in the course of normal investigations but has no particular claims concerning the subject matter of any discipline. Second, it is a matter of dispute whether the falsification methodology gives an accurate picture of the development of science. The "paradigm-shifting" approach of Thomas Kuhn (1970) suggests that changes in scientific approach come in sharp, discrete changes and not by the orderly process of falsification of hypotheses. Both considerations suggest that an expectation formation theory must stand on its own merits and cannot claim support from another discipline.

A third criticism of Muth's concept focuses on the role of learning. According to Muth's hypothesis, individuals calculate the expected values of key variables on the basis of the *true* probability distributions for the system. However, no description is given of how individuals actually find or learn about these probability distributions.

Benjamin Friedman (1979), Stephen De Canio (1979), and others have argued that typical "learning" processes may not even lead in the long run to a system that follows Muth's hypothesis. Suppose that individuals initially have *incorrect* beliefs about the way the system actually works. These beliefs will, in turn, affect the actual operation of the system. Since actual outcomes will be affected by individuals' own original misperceptions, learning the truth about the system may be difficult. However, some models have been developed [e.g., Cyert and Degroot (1974)] in which a learning process converges to the rational expectations equilibrium, which indicates that the "nonconvergence" results may not be robust. Work by Feldman (1982) and Bray and Kreps (1981) suggests that if the learning process is general enough, convergence to the true model is likely to occur.

Learning behavior, in and of itself, is not sufficient to call into question the rational expectations hypothesis. If the economic system does not undergo any significant structural change, it is likely that economic actors will eventually understand the system. For example, if the learning period started at the turn of the century and the system remained essentially unchanged, convergence might well be expected to have occurred by now.

Learning behavior, however, is most interesting when there is continual structural change. It has been argued that structural changes are the economic facts of life as institutions constantly adapt, government agencies become more complex and take on different functions, and new economic actors appear on the scene. In these circumstances, how can someone seriously contend that individuals' expectations depend on the *true* probabilities governing the system? Another way to characterize this position is that it contends that most changes are unpredictable, irreversible, and structural changes.

At first glance this view seems eminently plausible. Who can deny that uncertainty and change is the way of life and that in these circumstances it is difficult to imagine individuals who always know the true structure of a system? A careful examination of this position, however, raises some doubts about its persuasiveness.

An important distinction to make in discussing this topic is between *stable deterministic* (SD) systems and *stable stochastic* (SS) systems. An SD system may be disturbed from time to time but will always return to a stationary equilibrium – in other words, the system will settle down to a state of rest and remain there until a new shock hits it.

An SS system, however, is always in flux. Shocks are continually impinging on the system and it never settles down to a particular state. However, the shocks that impinge on the system follow stable probability laws. Consider a model of an agricultural commodity with the weather as the primary source of uncertainty. For simplicity, assume that there are only two types of weather – good and bad. The weather for next season is never totally predictable, but farmers observe certain patterns.

Specifically, rational farmers note that historically, if there is good weather this season, the probability of good weather next season (p) is high. Bad weather this season has historically indicated a high probability (q) of bad weather next season. Although the weather is unpredictable, it can be characterized by two simple parameters of its probability distribution – p and q. The fortunes of this agricultural system may fluctuate dramatically from year to year – there may be prolonged spells of bad weather – but as long as the shocks follow stable probability laws, the system can potentially be described as being in a stable, stochastic equilibrium.

Much of the appeal of the view that changes are unpredictable, irreversible, and structural comes from an implicit assumption that many equilibrium systems are of the stable deterministic type where change is rare, and thus it is thought that systems should almost always be in equilibrium. This habit of thinking equates equilibrium with the idea of a system at rest and is a hard habit to shake. Stable stochastic systems, however, are always in flux, and it is not immediately evident that most systems cannot be described by probability laws.

An important question for positive economics is whether economic systems, at most times, can be described as stable stochastic systems. This question can be approached on both a philosophical and a practical level. On the philosophical level, the question is similar to whether there truly exists structural change that could not be characterized ex ante by probability distributions. For example, Sargent and Wallace (1976) argue that it is difficult to even talk about shifts in the conduct of policy. If individuals can assign probabilities to potential policies, then any actual policy is just a realization from the probability distribution over policies. The actual policy chosen may have had a low probability of occurring but should this be seen as a "shift" in policy? This question can best be left for professional philosophers.

The practical question is clearer: Can economic science make progress by assuming that, at most times, economic systems can be characterized as being of the stable stochastic mode? The phrase "at most times" is added because even the strongest advocates of the rational expectations hypothesis believe that the hypothesis may not be appropriate for times of radical structural change. Posed in this way, the normal operation of economic science may be able to provide an answer to this question.

In all fairness to the critics of the rational expectations hypothesis, it is proper to remark on some weak arguments made in support of the hypothesis. For example, Kantor (1979) suggests that rational expectations are equivalent to profit-maximizing expectations for individual agents. More generally, rational expectations have been viewed as the natural consequence of either profit- or utility-maximizing behavior.

Once the case for rational expectations is made by appealing to maximizing behavior, it is legitimate to inquire into the constraints that individuals face. If information were truly free, only the limits of the Heisenberg Uncertainty Principle could prevent the rational expectations hypothesis from being converted into the assumption of perfect foresight. If information is scarce and can only be acquired at some cost, it is important to know the specific nature of the cost function to determine whether Muthian rationality emerges as the solution to a constrained maximization problem. Depending on the specification of the cost function, many different expectation schemes could be "rational." Because knowledge of these costs is so limited, it does not appear useful to base a theory of rational behavior solely on the benefit–cost principle of gathering information. This is not to say that arbitrage considerations may not, in some situations, lead to behavior corresponding to Muthian rationality. Indeed, this may be possible in some cases. However, as a general principle, it is unlikely that Muthian rationality would necessarily emerge as an optimal solution to a cost–benefit problem.

Finally, there are certain questions for which a knowledge of the diversity of individual behavior is important. If, for example, the need for a mandatory social insurance system is being analyzed, it is not enough to argue that, on average, individuals use probability theory correctly. We may be interested precisely in those individuals who do not evaluate probabilities correctly. Questions relating to the best strategy for constructing positive economic models (particularly aggregate models) are not the only ones that should concern economists.

Survey data and rational expectations

Rather than resorting to philosophical arguments to determine the best approach to economic model building, an empiricist would want to examine any available direct evidence on the individual's expectations. There exist data on expectations that have been derived from a number of different surveys. These survey data provide information on expectations in several areas, including forecasts for inflation rates, interest rates, and sales.

Recent years have witnessed the birth of a minor econometric growth industry devoted to examining this survey evidence and, in particular, testing for Muthian rationality. Before discussing the tests that have been applied, we should note that most of the tests focus on an aggregate or average response to a survey question. Individual responses exhibit considerable variation; by implication, not every individual survey response can be a conditional expectation based on the same information. This diversity of opinion leaves room for some individuals to arbitrage markets even when the average opinion is inconsistent with rational expectations. It also has important implications for market efficiency, which are pursued in Chapter 3.

The econometric literature on testing for rationality is a bit untidy because of all the seemingly different tests that have been employed. There are basically four different tests that have been used extensively. Letting $_{t-k}X_t^\epsilon$ signify the expectation reported in the survey for a variable X_t made at time $t - k$, the four tests for rationality can be outlined.

1. Unbiasedness. The survey expectation should be an unbiased predictor of the variable. That is, a regression of the form

$$X_t = a + b_{t-k}X_t^\epsilon + \epsilon_t$$

should yield coefficient estimates $a = 0$ and $b = 1$.

2. Efficiency. The survey expectation should use information about the past history of the variable in the same way that the variable actually evolves through time. That is, in the two regressions,

$$_{t-1}X_t^\epsilon = a_1 X_{t-1} + a_2 X_{t-2} + \cdots + a_n X_{t-n} + \epsilon_t$$

$$X_t = b_1 X_{t-1} + b_2 X_{t-2} + \cdots + b_n X_{t-n} + u_t$$

it must be true that $a_i = b_i$ for all i.

3. Forecast error unpredictability. The forecast error, that is, the difference between the survey expectation and the actual realization of the variable, should be uncorrelated with *any* information available at the time the forecast is made.

4. Consistency. When forecasts are given for the same variable at different times in the future, the forecasts should be consistent with one another. For example, in the regressions,

$$
\begin{aligned}
_{t-2}X_t^\epsilon &= c_1 \, _{t-2}X_{t-1}^\epsilon + c_2 X_{t-2} \\
&\quad + \cdots c_n X_{t-n} X_{t-n} + \epsilon_t
\end{aligned}
$$

$$
\begin{aligned}
_{t-1}X_t^\epsilon &= a_1 X_{t-1} + a_2 X_{t-2} \\
&\quad + \cdots a_n X_{t-n} + u_t
\end{aligned}
$$

it must be true that $c_i = a_i$ for all i.

Although these tests may appear to be quite dissimilar, they are simply different devices to test whether the reported survey expectations are consistent with being conditional expectations. In fact, all the tests are simply different ways of testing properties of conditional expectations. Consider, for example, the efficiency test and suppose that $a_1 \neq b_1$. Subtracting the first equation from the second yields the expression

$$
X_t - \, _{t-1}X_t^\epsilon = \text{forecast error} = (a_1 - b_1)X_{t-1} \qquad (1.8)
$$

Since, by hypothesis $a_1 \neq b_1$, this implies that the forecast error is correlated with X_{t-1}, which violates the orthogonality property of conditional expectations as long as X_{t-1} is contained in the information set. Although it would be desirable for any expectation mechanism to satisfy at least some of these four properties, conditional expectations must satisfy all of them.

Implementing these tests is far from mechanical, and the econometric results have varied across data and investigators. To gain an appreciation of the issues that arise in practice, one finds it instructive to review the history of three testing episodes based on the Livingston inflation forecasts, the Goldsmith–Nagan interest rate forecasts, and the Commerce Department sales forecast data.

Livingston data

One would not necessarily expect to see extensive references to the *Philadelphia Bulletin* and *Inquirer* in academic journals, particularly when other prominent papers such as the *New York Times* and *Washington Post* are rarely mentioned. The prominence of the Philadelphia papers can be attributed to the surveys that columnist Joseph Livingston collected and published over the years on inflation expectations. Early users of the series did not test for rationality. Turnovsky (1970) explored which of several common forecasting rules (adaptive, regressive, etc.) could best account for the reported series, whereas Gibson (1972) used the series to explain movements in nominal interest rates.

The first person to test the Livingston series for rationality was Pesando (1975). Over the sample period 1959–69 Pesando rejected the hypothesis of rationality principally because the consistency test was violated. The data Pesando used for these tests were aggregated from the individual responses by Livingston himself.

Carlson (1977) argued that Livingston's aggregation procedure may have introduced some biases into the inflation forecasts and calculated a new series. He found that both the efficiency and consistency tests were violated and hence concluded that the Livingston series was not Muth rational.

Mullineaux (1978) criticized the econometric techniques employed by both Pesando and Carlson. Using the Carlson version of the Livingston data, he found that his tests of Muth rationality did not reject the hypothesis for the period 1959–69. Although the Carlson-adjusted Livingston series may have passed Mullineaux's tests, it was not the best predictor available for future inflation. Pearce (1979) found that univariate time-series models could yield better inflation predictions than the Livingston data. This meant that the series could not be fully Muth rational; some past information was not exploited efficiently by the Livingston forecasters.

All these tests relied on aggregate responses that were derived from individual responses to the survey. Figlewski and Wachtel (1981) used the individual data to test alternative theories of expectation formation. Using a sample containing over seventy-one forecasters, they found that they could easily reject the unbiasedness condition. In addition, past forecast errors were also significant explanatory factors of current forecast errors, indicating that the orthogonality principle was also violated.

The results of the extensive research on the Livingston data are, at best, mixed. The verdict on Muth rationality for the aggregate series depends on the time period examined, the econometric techniques, and the aggregation procedure. The one study on the individual responses clearly rejected the rationality hypothesis.

Goldsmith–Nagan Letter

Benjamin Friedman (1980) used interest rate forecasts from the *Goldsmith–Nagan Bond and Money Letter* to test for Muth rationality. The *Letter* provided a rich set of forecasts of interest rates, including forecasts one and two quarters ahead of both representative long- and short-term rates.

Friedman reported that the results of his tests were mixed to unfavorable. The forecasts were not unbiased, the two-quarter ahead forecasts did not efficiently exploit past interest rate movements, the one- and two-quarter forecasts were not always consistent, and forecast errors for long-term interest rates were correlated with available macroeconomic information. It should be emphasized that not all the series failed the rationality tests and that forecasts of short-term rates fared better than those of long-term rates.

One interesting result was that forecast errors for long-term interest rates were uncorrelated with available money supply information, although they were correlated with other macroeconomic information. Friedman attributed this to the monetarist emphasis in the financial press. This, of course, must be an enlightened monetarism; a crude version might not fare as well.

Sales expectation data

Hirsch and Lovell (1969) tested for rationality of sales expectations by using Commerce Department data. As Lovell (1976:404) described their findings, "Firms do not report forecasts appropriate for use as certainty equivalents in linear decision rules; they do not succeed in taking optimal advantage of all the information available at the time they make their forecasts." This conclusion was based on both aggregated and disaggregated data. They raised the possibility that the reported sales expectations may not reflect firms' true expectations but, instead, be simply the projections of the persons responsible for filling out the forms requested by the government.

A more recent study by Irvine (1981) that used an extended sample period for the aggregate data found more support for Muth rationality. Specifically, from the period 1962–73, the sales expectations passed the unbiasedness tests and most of the orthogonality tests. Starting in 1973, however, there were persistent errors and thus over the entire period up to 1976 the rationality hypothesis was rejected. Irvine argued that the break in the series in 1973 corresponded to sharp structural changes that were induced in the economy by the first major Organization of Petroleum Exporting Countries (OPEC) shock. Unfortunately, the aggregate series ended in 1976, preventing an investigation of whether reported sales expectations returned to "rationality."

The issue raised by Irvine concerning possible structural change has important implications for testing for rationality. In almost all studies, investigators break the sample up into different periods and test for rationality in each period. One of the reasons that this seems to be a plausible procedure is that the stochastic processes governing the economic series are thought perhaps to differ over the subsamples. After all, if they did not, breaking up the sample would only result in less efficient tests. However, if the stochastic processes do change and the investigator either fails to separate the sample properly or allow for even a learning period of short duration, the hypothesis of Muthian rationality may be rejected. This can occur when, for the most part, the survey evidence is actually consistent with Muthian rationality.

The rather mixed evidence from all these diverse surveys does not necessarily imply that the rational expectations hypothesis will be of only limited use for economics. There are essentially three reasons for discounting some of the findings of the surveys. First, and most simply, people may not do what they say. There is no reason that this basic insight to human nature need not apply here. Second, as previously discussed, surveys are used to determine average expectations but in many market situations the marginal participant plays the key role. Particularly in markets in which transactions costs are low, a few sophisticated arbitrageurs could make the markets function as predicted by the rational expectations hypothesis, even when the average expectations were biased and inefficient. Finally, as Prescott (1977) has stressed, there is only limited value in testing assumptions:

> The rational expectations paradigm may be considered in the same spirit as the maximizing assumption, once the subject of much debate in economics but now considered to be fundamental. The rational expectations assumption augmented the maximizing assumption by hypothesizing that agents use their information sets efficiently when maximizing. Like utility, expectations are not observed and *surveys cannot be used to test the rational expectations hypothesis*. One can only test if some theory, whether it incorporates rational expectations or, for that matter, irrational expectations, is or is not consistent with observations. (1977:30)

Prescott somewhat understates the value of the survey data. Researchers have not used the survey data to evaluate all the implications of the rational expectations hypothesis but simply to test if the hypothesis bears any resemblance to actual reported expectations. If every survey (including those that examined individual responses) revealed that expectations were totally at odds with the realized time series, then an unbiased scientific investigator would not put much faith in a research program based on rational expectations. However, the survey data do *not* settle the question and an examination of the rational expectations hypothesis must go beyond these tests.

Plan of the survey

With neither the philosophical arguments nor the survey evidence pointing to any dramatic conclusions, it is necessary to follow Prescott's suggestion and examine whether the rational expectations hypothesis has delivered any theoretical or empirical insights in various areas of economics. The remaining chapters of the book do precisely that. They explore the contributions of the rational expectations hypothesis in diverse areas of economic thought: macroeconomics, financial markets, and models of microeconomic behavior.

Although Muth's original examples may have been from microeconomics, it is the area of macroeconomics that witnessed the explosion of interest in the hypothesis. Part of this interest originated because of the seeming failures of conventional macroeconomics in the 1970s. Stagflation and persistent inflation created a receptive environment for new ideas in the field.

Another important factor was the seemingly shocking propositions that emerged out of the new macroeconomics of rational expectations. One of these propositions asserted that predictable behavior on the part of monetary authorities would have absolutely no effect on the level of output or other real variables in a typical macroeconomic system. Although this proposition caught many economists' attention, as we will see in Chapter 2, it is subject to many limitations. There is, however, some interesting empirical work that lends at least some plausibility to this view. In Chapter 2 the evidence on this issue and the broader question of rational expectations and the supply side of the economy are treated in detail.

Contributions of the rational expectations hypothesis in macroeconomics were not limited to the topic of aggregate supply. The issues raised in these discussions touched on the very basis of the use of empirical econometric models. Essentially, the consistent application of the rational expectations hypothesis called into question a key assumption implicit in the use of all economic models. Simply put, it appears that the equations of economic models will not remain invariant to policy changes; or, in other words, economic models will change as different policy situations are contemplated. The proper use of economic models in these circumstances is one of the topics treated in Chapter 3. Two other topics are also dealt with that have interested macroeconomic scholars.

Models in which only some of the sectors exhibit rational behavior have been suggested by some economists as a possible compromise with rational expectations. For many economists the assumption of rational expectations has seemed to be more suited to fluid financial markets than to labor markets where arbitrage is more difficult. The marriage between a rational financial sector and a nonrational labor market is studied in Chapter 3.

The second topic in the chapter focuses on the issue of the best way to conduct economic policy when agents have rational expectations. Some interesting developments have recently challenged the "optimal control" view of policy that was very popular in the past decade. The new ideas concern the *inconsistency* of policies or, speaking loosely, the possibility that the government will have an incentive to renege on promises in the future. This issue has also been linked with the traditional topic of the proper role of rules versus discretion in the conduct of economic policy. Both the problem of inconsistency and the link to the rules and discretion debate are treated in detail.

Rational expectations in financial markets have been studied for some time now under the name of "efficient markets." In Chapter 4 we first explore the microfoundations of the efficient market ideas, in particular, the recent work by Grossman and Stiglitz (1976, 1980), which suggests certain problems with the conventional notion of efficient markets. After reviewing these issues, we turn to an examination of the empirical evidence pertaining to the efficient markets model. Tests of the efficient markets hypothesis are necessarily joint tests of market efficiency and of a particular model chosen to specify the determination of equilibrium returns.

Many of the early tests of the efficient markets model were based on the hypothesis that expected returns were constant. The capital-asset-pricing model, developed in the finance literature, was an alternative model of the process that generates equilibrium returns. Early tests of market efficiency using both paradigms appeared to confirm the efficient markets model.

Recent work, however, has been critical of these models of the return-generating process. An important development was the introduction of the "volatility" tests. These tests appeared to indicate that prices of financial instruments fluctuate too much to be consistent with existing models of equilibrium returns. In an independent development the existing tests of capital-asset-pricing model were discovered to be much weaker tests of the model than previously believed. Finally, there was other evidence that seemed to be inconsistent with simple models of the return-generating process.

Rather than rejecting the rational expectations hypothesis, there has been considerable effort devoted to developing alternative models of equilibrium returns. One of the more promising models involves discount rates that vary systematically with consumption opportunities. This model is explored at the end of the chapter.

The examples Muth utilized in his article were drawn from agricultural economics, which is examined in Chapter 5, as a paradigm case of microeconomic modeling. Until recently, Nerlove's adaptive expectations hypothesis appeared to satisfy demands for a theory of expectations in this area. We illustrate, however, the procedures that can be used to test the rational expectations hypothesis in empirical models and present evidence from a particular case study. The use of the rational expectations hypothesis is also explored in another microeconomic model to study the role of capital gains in the market for housing. The potential for more work by using rational expectations in empirical microeconomic models is great, but the number of existing studies is, at this time, quite limited.

The final chapter pulls together and examines whether the insights gathered in the survey from the experiences in microeconomics, financial theory, and macroeconomics justify continued interest and work in the area of rational expectations. The "test" that will be used is whether thinking in substantive areas has changed because of influence from the rational expectations approach. As the survey indicates, it is difficult to find an area of economic thought that has not been affected.

2

Inflation and unemployment

Although counterfactual history of thought is a highly speculative business, one may plausibly argue that without extensive work on the rational expectations hypothesis by macroeconomic theorists, John Muth's ideas would not be anywhere near as popular as they are today. Robert E. Lucas's several seminal papers in the early 1970s took Muth's concept and pushed it to the forefront of current economic thought. The background for these papers was the growing professional interest in the formation and effects of inflationary expectations, a topic that was brought forcefully to the attention of the profession by Phelps (1970) and Friedman (1968). Any discussion of the rational expectations hypothesis in macroeconomics must therefore begin with the Phelps–Friedman "natural rate" revolution.

Until the work of Phelps and Friedman, the Phillips curve was the established doctrine linking unemployment and inflation. Over two decades ago A. W. Phillips (1958) noticed a striking inverse relationship between the British unemployment and inflation rates. This empirical observation became known as the Phillips curve and gave rise to both an extensive body of empirical studies attempting to replicate this finding for other periods and countries and the notion that there was an exploitable "trade-off" between inflation and unemployment. Policymakers could achieve a lower unemployment rate but only at the expense of a higher inflation rate or could achieve a lower inflation rate but only by incurring higher unemployment.

The theoretical justification for the Phillips curve was, on the surface, quite straightforward. When unemployment was relatively low, firms found it hard to find workers and tended to bid up wages – whereas in slack labor markets there was less upward pressure. In the unionized labor markets – accounting for less than one-third of the U.S. labor force – a similar story was told. In tight labor markets a union strike could be devastating because firms would be unable to recruit additional labor and thus would lose sales. Firms therefore would tend to accede to unions' demands, thus leading to wage inflation in periods of low unemployment. If prices simply are a markup on wages, there will be a direct connection between unemployment and inflation – the observed Phillips curve. The idea of a stable trade-off between unemployment and inflation gained popular appeal, although Lipsey (1960) and Perry (1966), among others, recognized that factors besides the unemployment rate could influence the course of wage inflation.

Phelps and Friedman argued that a stable and permanent trade-off between unemployment and inflation was an illusion; in the long run only one rate of unemployment (the "natural rate") was possible to sustain without experiencing an acceleration or deceleration of inflation. As Friedman argued in his presidential address to the American Economic Association, there is no stable relationship between inflation and unemployment, only one between *unanticipated inflation* and unemployment. At the beginning of an inflationary period workers are slower than firms to recognize the full extent of the inflation, and therefore they think that the higher nominal wages being offered are actually higher real wages. With this apparent higher real wage, workers offer more labor services, people accept jobs rather than keep searching for better ones, and the unemployment rate falls. When workers realize they have misjudged the inflation rate, they will withdraw some of their labor, some workers will quit their jobs, and the unemployment rate will return to its "natural rate."

According to Friedman, there is a short-run trade-off between inflation and unemployment only because expectations of inflation are slow to adjust; since people cannot be "fooled" forever, there is no long-run relationship between inflation and unemployment. If the monetary authorities wish to keep the unemployment rate below its natural rate, they can do so by forcing the actual inflation rate to exceed the public's expected rate; in the long run this can only be accomplished by accelerating inflation. Unemployment can temporarily be brought down below the natural rate but only at the expense of a higher permanent inflation rate. Unemployment will have to exceed the natural rate for a period of time to reduce the inflation rate to its original level.

The natural-rate hypothesis still permitted policy options that concern inflation and unemployment. If expectations of inflation are formed by some type of learning mechanism, then it would be possible to pursue expansionary policies that temporarily lowered unemployment if the actual inflation rate exceeded the expected inflation rate. If inflationary expectations only gradually adjust to actual experience, as would be the case with the adaptive expectations concept developed by Cagan (1956), then policymakers could weigh the *temporary* employment gain against the losses from *permanently* higher inflation rates. Phelps (1972) and Hall (1976) explicitly discussed policy trade-offs within the natural-rate framework along these lines. The natural-rate hypothesis changed the terms on which unemployment and inflation policy could be conducted but still left a potential for an activist employment policy. As long as expectations of inflation adjust sluggishly to actual inflation experience, then by "fooling" the public, employment gains can be temporarily achieved. Friedman (1968), himself, spoke of the long period needed for inflationary expectations to adjust and even mentioned a figure of several decades.

Rational expectation theorists began with the natural-rate hypothesis but posed the following question: Why should participants in the economy be systematically "fooled" by the inflation rate? If one assumes that people are interested in maximizing their own welfare, they will try to make accurate forecasts of the inflation rate. This does not mean that people can perfectly predict the rate of inflation. It only indicates that they should utilize all readily available information in their forecasts, including proposed monetary policy and fiscal policy. The public's mistakes in predicting inflation should not have a systematic component because they could remove this component and improve their forecasts. Therefore the mistakes in predicting inflation will have to be random – mistakes can be made, but the public can never be systematically fooled about the inflation rate. Movements in the unemployment rate from its natural rate can still occur when mistakes are made in predicting inflation, but these errors must be of a random nature.

As pointed out by T. Sargent and N. Wallace (1976), the implication of this view for the potency of monetary policy is rather startling. Because the public watches the monetary authorities and anticipates their actions in predicting prices, it is only the *unanticipated* growth of the money supply that can make the actual inflation rate diverge from the expected inflation rate. In other words, any anticipated actions on the part of the monetary authorities will be incorporated into the public's expectations of inflation; because unemployment can only diverge from its natural rate when people are fooled about the inflation rate, it follows that systematic, anticipated monetary policy has no effect on output or employment. Only when the Federal Reserve System (Fed) has the money supply growing faster or more slowly than the public anticipates can it have an effect on the economy.

This brief introduction raises many questions. Are the theoretical propositions concerning the impotence of anticipated monetary policy robust to slight modifications of the models? Can mere random mistakes in predicting inflation lead to the prolonged business cycles that characterize the economy? Is there reasonable empirical evidence supporting any version of a rational expectations model of aggregate supply?

Our strategy for coming to grips with these issues will be first to present Lucas's (1977) cohesive account of the business cycle. This will set the stage for a discussion of the robustness of the theoretical propositions associated with "rational expectations," including issues relating to the neutrality of money, the informational structure of the economy, and the existence of nominal contracts. We will then turn to an examination of the question of the duration or persistence of business cycles and to an examination of the empirical evidence relating to rational expectation models of aggregate supply. Finally, the last section steps back from the formal models and discusses the alternative visions lying behind some of the rational expectation models and the Keynesian alternatives.

Lucas's account of the business cycle

On several occasions Lucas (1977, 1978b) has clearly outlined his view of the sources of business cycles and the meaning of fluctuations in unemployment. His analysis is based on a model in which individual, competitive agents make decisions with less than perfect information. These agents should be thought of as representative producers, producing a common good for the market. In this one good world the selling price of the individual agent's output can be identified with the real wage. Each day the agent wakes up, observes the selling price for his good, and decides on the number of hours he wants to work.

How should an individual respond to an increase in the selling price of his product? A complete answer to this question depends on whether the price change is perceived to be temporary or permanent. A permanent change in the selling price (which is equivalent, in this model, to a permanent increase in the real wage) should have little effect on employment. The evidence from the field of labor economics suggests that supply elasticities of labor with respect to the real wage are very low for primary workers. In other words, when real wages increase, primary workers still supply roughly the same amount of labor. Thus a perceived permanent change in the selling price of the product should not cause substantial employment changes.

For changes in prices that are perceived to be temporary, Lucas argues that employment will change dramatically. Consider a situation in which the selling price today is expected to be somewhat higher than in the future. It would pay for our producer to work more now and take his leisure at a later date when the opportunity cost of his time is lower. Conversely, when the selling price is perceived to be temporarily lower than usual, workers will take vacations because the price of leisure time is low. It makes sense, therefore, to think that labor supply may vary sharply when a worker is confronted with small, temporary fluctuations in his wage regardless of his response to a permanent increase in his wage. It is at least conceivable that employment fluctuations occur because workers are essentially speculators who are taking their leisure time when they think it costs the least.

What evidence is available on the elasticity of labor supply with respect to temporary changes in wages? Quoting Lucas:

> Systematic evidence at the aggregate level was obtained by Rapping and myself (1970); Ghez and Becker (1975) reached the same conclusion at a disaggregative level. The small premiums required to induce workers to shift holidays and vacations (take Monday off instead of Saturday, two weeks in March rather than in August) point to the same conclusion, and this "casual" evidence is somewhat more impressive because of its probabilistic simplicity: holidays are *known* to be transitory. (1977:16–17)

With a high degree of substitutability of leisure over time, small, temporary changes in wages can, in principle, induce sharp shifts in employment.

The response of workers to temporary changes in wages is a very important part of Lucas's story. Lucas wants to explain business fluctuations within models in which labor markets clear – that is, he wishes to avoid any notion of "involuntary unemployment." In other words, workers should always be on their labor supply curves. The supply of labor must vary during a business cycle even though observed fluctuations of wages and prices are often rather moderate. It is, therefore, essential for the theory that small fluctuations in wages or prices can cause sharp movements in labor supply. If the supply of labor were insensitive to movements in real wages, then business fluctuations could not be explained by small movements in wages or prices.

Before proceeding any further, we should stress that this view of labor supply allows for certain types of fiscal policies to have substantial macroeconomic effects. Temporary increases or decreases in income tax rates should induce sharp responses in labor supply by temporarily changing the after-tax return to labor. Permanent tax rate changes, on the other hand, should have much more limited effects on labor supply.

When our worker wakes up in the morning and observes a higher price for his product, no omniscient economist is there to tell him whether it is a permanent or only a temporary increase. The worker must determine how much of the increase in his price can be ascribed to permanent factors and how much of it is only a transitory phenomenon. The individual producer faces what the engineers call a ''signal-extraction'' problem. He must decompose the change in his selling price into permanent and temporary components.

How should the individual do this? It seems plausible that he should rely on his past experience. If most past changes in his selling price have been permanent ones, then it is reasonable to assume that the current one is permanent. On the other hand, if most changes in prices have, in the past, been temporary, then the individual should treat the current price change as mostly temporary. In more technical language, we can relate his inference to the relative variances of the permanent and temporary components of his selling price. If most of the variance of his selling price can be accounted for by movements in the permanent component of his price, the individual will treat the current price change as mostly reflecting permanent factors.

In the typical situation in which there have been experiences of both movements in prices, the individual will attribute some of a price increase to permanent factors and some to temporary factors. His labor supply will vary only to that portion of the change in his price that the individual perceives to be temporary. Therefore, unless a producer has some special insight that allows him to distinguish temporary from permanent price changes, he will generally supply more labor when his price increases and supply less labor when his price decreases.

As tastes change, new products are invented, and technology advances, we would naturally expect some producers to prosper and others to suffer losses. Some individuals will face increased prices for their products, whereas others will face decreased prices. Those producers with the good fortune of facing higher prices will supply more labor and those with bad fortune will supply less. Individual fortunes may be quite varied in this world, but there is no reason to expect *economy-wide* changes in fortunes. A better mousetrap may put the mice poison manufacturers out of business, but there is no reason to believe that the whole mice-eradication industry should collapse. In other words, we have no reason to believe that business cycles will occur in the world just described. To allow for the possibility of business cycles, we must introduce another type of uncertainty into the system, *nominal price* uncertainty.

Thus far we have assumed that the representative producer had no difficulty in ascertaining the real price for his product. Although it is true that he will always be able to ascertain the nominal or money price of his good, in a world in which the aggregate price level is uncertain, there are problems in determining the *real* price. Economic agents should be interested in the purchasing power of a unit of their labor, not merely the dollar payment. When the aggregate price level is uncertain, the individual producer must face another "signal-extraction" problem. The producer experiences a change in his nominal selling price but must infer the change in his real price; that is, he must decide how much of a change in his price is due to general inflation and how much to a relative change in his price.

The representative producer will solve this inference problem in the same manner as before – relying on his past experience with price movements. If most changes in his price were due to general inflation, the producer will attribute the current price change to mere inflation. If most price changes have been changes in relative prices, then he will view this price change as a relative price change. In other words, if most of the movements in prices occur because of fluctuations in the aggregate price level, the representative producer will suspect that most changes in his price reflect general inflation rather than relative price changes. If aggregate prices are relatively stable, then movements in prices will be perceived to be changes in relative prices.

It is essential for this analysis that the individual does not have *too much* information. If a producer had a report of all the other prices in the economy, he could quickly calculate a price index and determine the average price level in the economy. Our individual producers do not possess this much information and hence cannot distinguish between a movement in *all* prices from a movement only in their own price. Thus they are forced to rely on their past experience to try to decompose the current price change. Many critics argue that this is an untenable assumption. The economy is awash with information – newspapers and networks bombard us with current statistics. What is Lucas's justification for this assumption?

Fundamentally, gathering *accurate* economy-wide information takes time, money, and resources. Individuals, of course, have access to some economy-wide information through newspapers, consulting services, and so on. Still it is difficult to get *precise* information on short notice, and as Lucas argues, profit opportunities depend on being able to react quickly to possible "bargains" in the economy. By the time an individual producer waits for an accurate economy-wide measure, his profit opportunity may be gone. Moreover, Lucas argues that most uncertainties that individual producers face are related to developments in their own industry and not general macroeconomic trends. (Will my rival undercut me? Will my input costs get out of hand?) For any particular producer, aggregate price uncertainty constitutes only a very small part of his overall uncertainty, and it is not, on the margin, worth the extra cost to ascertain the aggregate price level accurately. In other words, producers must respond quickly to possible profit opportunities, and it probably is not worth the cost to obtain accurate economy-wide information.

In principle, it should be possible to test alternative assumptions about the information sets available to producers. Although there has been some interesting work along these lines by Pauls (1980), the need to use industry price indices necessarily makes inference about situations of individual firms a difficult task. Nonetheless, this is a fundamental aspect of Lucas's work and deserves further examination.

With the possibility of a confusion between aggregate and relative price levels, economy-wide business fluctuations can easily develop. Suppose that the "money stock" increases unexpectedly, which leads to an unanticipated increase in the general price level. Individual producers would, depending on their past experience with inflation, attribute part of their price change to aggregate price change and part to a relative price change. To the extent that the perceived relative price change is thought to be temporary, employment will increase. Each producer may only work a little more, but in the aggregate, total employment can increase quite a bit because everyone is simultaneously deciding to work a little more. Recessions and decreases in employment occur when the aggregate price level is lower than anticipated, and workers perceive this to be, in part, a temporary fall in their relative price. As intertemporal leisure speculators, they take their vacation now, and the aggregate "holiday" becomes a recession.

In countries that have had volatile aggregate price levels (Latin American countries, e.g.) producers will view most price movements as aggregate price changes so that monetary shocks will not cause large fluctuations in output and employment. On the other hand, in countries with stable price levels unanticipated aggregate price movements will be viewed as being mainly changes in relative prices, and economic agents will incorrectly assume that the current price increase is a relative price increase. In a country with a volatile inflation history workers will not be fooled that easily, and output will not respond very much to unanticipated inflation. This general prediction from the theory of signal extraction is supported in extreme cases from data on cross-country experiences with inflation as Lucas's (1973) study indicates.

This theory has an interesting policy implication. If we start in an economy with a stable inflation history, policymakers can engineer "booms" rather easily by causing some unanticipated inflation. If they continue with this policy, the inflation rate will become more volatile. The greater volatility in the inflation rate will make it difficult to engage in similar policies in the future as agents will be less likely to respond to this type of engineered inflation. They will learn to distrust their price changes as signals of relative price change. Thus a little "trickery" is possible at first, but the government will soon find that it will be increasingly difficult to engage in future trickery.

Unlike Friedman's account of the business cycle, there is no asymmetry between workers and firms with regard to unanticipated inflation. In Lucas's thinking, firms and workers should be considered a coherent group. The firm and its workers together experience price fluctuations for their product and, as a unit, must face the signal-extraction problem. If the price of the firm's product is believed to be temporarily low, then the value of the workers' marginal product will also be temporarily low. It is in the joint interest of workers and firms to let the workers take "holidays" at this time. Depending on the institutional arrangements between workers and firms, this holiday may appear to the untutored eye as an involuntary layoff. Meltzer (1978:170) is quite explicit on this point: "Teachers are not typically regarded as 'involuntarily unemployed' in the summer; construction workers are not involuntarily unemployed when it rains; industrial workers are not involuntarily unemployed in mild cycles of short duration." Formal models along these lines have been developed by Azariadis (1975) and Bailey (1974). Although Lucas (1977) views the institutional arrangements between workers and firms as an interesting problem, he argues that for business cycle theory we may properly abstract from these considerations. In essence, we need not model the worker and firm separately but can retain our model of a representative producer.

One missing link in our story is the explanation for movements in the general price level. Given that unanticipated movements in the general price level can cause business fluctuations, what causes movements in aggregate prices? The answer, perhaps not surprisingly, is money. Lucas argues that the evidence linking long-term movements in prices to money is strong but that over shorter periods the link between the price level and the money stock is not that tight. In an interesting dialectical twist, Lucas argues that the loose short-run link between past money growth and prices actually gives support to his theory. If the link between previous money growth and prices were very close, agents would simply look up the appropriate monetary statistics and calculate the corresponding general price level. In that case there could be no unanticipated inflation and hence no business cycles. It is crucial, therefore, that previous monetary statistics be only an imperfect indicator of future developments in the aggregate price level. In some sense it is only because the lags from money to prices are variable that business cycles can actually occur, as knowledge of the past money stock is then not sufficient to predict the current price level perfectly.

Finally, changes in real interest rates can also affect employment. If interest rates are temporarily high, it pays someone to work now, put the proceeds in the bank, and use the interest income to reduce labor supply in the future. This is just another mechanism by which workers can speculate over the best time to enjoy their leisure. When should interest rates be temporarily high? High interest rates are a sign that output is valued more in the present than in the future. A war is a good example of a situation in which resources are temporarily valued higher than usual. We would thus expect, according to this theory, sharp increases in labor supply during wartime. It is interesting to note that this gives a completely different explanation for a wartime boom. Traditionally, involuntary unemployed resources are brought to work by changes in demand. Here, temporary changes in aggregate demand induce changes in labor supply.

Our account of employment and output fluctuations only explains employment fluctuations and not why the *unemployment rate* should fluctuate. To economists who maintain that involuntary unemployment exists and is a fundamental part of the business cycle, this aspect of Lucas's work is particularly troubling. Robert Solow (1980), for example, in his American Economic Association presidential address finds it utterly implausible that high unemployment rates arise from workers who are speculating over the right time to enjoy their leisure. To Solow, massive unemployment means that labor markets do not clear and that there is pervasive excess supply of labor. In simple terms, workers cannot get jobs at the prevailing wage. Layoffs are not merely disguised vacations but represent involuntary separations from desired jobs. This, of course, has been the traditional view of unemployment fluctuations over the business cycle.

Lucas dismisses the evidence based on the unemployment survey as indicating that any excess supply of labor exists. In Lucas's model, if a worker perceives a low price and does not work, he might respond to a survey by saying that he would like to work at his "normal" wage. Because the normal wage currently exceeds the existing wage, there is no evidence that work cannot be found at the *current* wage. As Lucas (1978b:354) writes, "there is an involuntary element in all unemployment, in the sense that no one chooses bad luck over good; there is also a voluntary element in all unemployment, in the sense that however miserable one's current work options, one can always choose to accept them."

Pressed on this point, Lucas (1978b:354) offers a somewhat philosophical justification for his views. Unemployment statistics do not indicate that disequilibrium exists in the labor market.

> Involuntary unemployment is not a fact or a phenomenon which it is the task of theorists to explain. It is, on the contrary a theoretical construct which Keynes introduced in the hope that it would be helpful in discovering a correct explanation for a genuine phenomenon: large-scale fluctuations in measured, total unemployment. Is it the task of modern theoretical economics to "explain" the theoretical constructs of our predecessors?

This, of course, is a position that is characteristic of Milton Friedman's positive economics. Assumptions are always "simple" and hence incorrect, and the test of the theory comes in its predictions. An assumption that deviates substantially from reality, however, could never produce a good theory, which is the position that Solow and the "nonequilibrium" theorists take with respect to the market-clearing assumption. Looking at an unemployment rate of 9 percent, Solow sees involuntary unemployment and thus dismisses Lucas's theory out of hand. Lucas contends that "involuntary unemployment" is a theoretical construct and should only be judged in relation to a complete theory of the business cycle. In Lucas's view involuntary unemployment is neither an obvious nor useful concept. The crucial question for Lucas is whether his equilibrium theory can provide a more satisfactory account of business cycles than the traditional Keynesian alternative.

How robust are the invariance propositions?

Some of the most well-known propositions associated with rational expectations and macroeconomics actually derive from models that are much simpler in structure than Lucas's model and focus more on the demand side. Perhaps the most famous of these is the so-called invariance proposition, which asserts that any predictable part of the money supply should have *no effect* on output, employment, or any other real variables in the economy. Only *unpredictable* money supply changes can have an effect on output. In particular, it makes no difference for the behavior of output and employment whether the Fed follows an activist policy (e.g., increasing the money growth rate during a recession and decreasing it during a boom) or sticks to a constant money growth rule. The behavior of the price level and the inflation rate will be affected by both anticipated and unanticipated parts of the money supply but only those movements that were not anticipated can affect output.

The invariance proposition can be seen within a simple model based on the work of Sargent and Wallace (1976). The model has three components: an aggregate demand relation, an aggregate supply relation, and a money supply rule. Let us consider each of these in turn.

The aggregate demand for output will take a very simple form. Fiscal policy will be assumed to be held constant, and monetary policy will be the only policy variable affecting the demand for output. For expositional purposes only, the velocity of money will also be a constant. With these assumptions, the aggregate demand for output can be written, in logs, as

$$M_t + \overline{V}_t = P_t + y_t \qquad \text{aggregate demand} \qquad (2.1)$$

where

M_t = log of the money supply
$\bar{V_t}$ = log of the (constant) velocity of money
P_t = log of the price level
y_t = log of real output

This equation, of course, is nothing but the simple equation of exchange, written in logs. The assumption of a constant velocity of money requires that the demand for money is not responsive to the interest rate, but this assumption is not crucial for the subsequent analysis.

The aggregate supply curve is based on an interpretation of Lucas's work and hence has come to be known as the Lucas supply equation. Output will deviate from full employment or capacity output (y_p) only when actual prices differ from those that the public anticipates. Again, in logs,

$$y_t = y_p + \beta(P_t - {}_{t-1}P_t^\epsilon) \qquad \text{Lucas supply equation} \qquad (2.2)$$

where

y_p = full employment output
${}_{t-1}P_t^\epsilon$ = log of the price level that the public expects
will occur in time t viewed from period $t - 1$.

The public is assumed to form expectations about the price level that will prevail in period t at the end of period $t - 1$. If the actual price level exceeds the anticipated price level, representative producers will attribute part of this to an increase in their relative price and output will be above trend. On the other hand, if the price level is below the level anticipated, producers will, in part, believe that relative prices are low and output will fall below its trend value.

Assuming the money supply and price expectations are fixed or predetermined, we can present a simple graphical analysis in p-y space. In Figure 2.1 the aggregate demand curve is downward sloping, reflecting the fact that with a given money stock, higher prices must lead to lower output to keep nominal demand constant. The aggregate supply curve, drawn for a given level of expected prices, is upward sloping, reflecting the fact that at higher price levels the

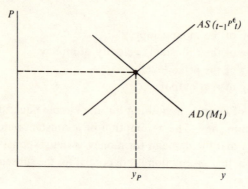

Figure 2.1 Price and output determination.

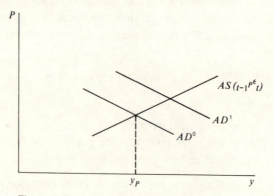

Figure 2.2 An increase in the money supply with no change in expectations.

gap between actual and expected prices increases, leading to higher levels of output. If price expectations did not change when the money supply increased, then output and prices would both increase as shown in Figure 2.2.

In Figure 2.2 the increase in the money supply shifts the aggregate demand curve from AD^0 to AD^1, thereby raising prices and output. Although this result is typical of most macroeconomic models, it is not, in general, consistent with rational expectations.

In rational expectations models, price expectations are not fixed or predetermined but respond to anticipated movements in the money supply. To illustrate this, one must provide a monetary rule that is utilized by the policy authorities. An example of a rule might be the following:

$$M_t = \alpha_1 y_{t-1} + \epsilon_t \qquad \text{money supply rule} \qquad (2.3)$$

where

$$E(\epsilon_t | I_{t-1}) = 0$$

The money supply in time t is a function of the last period's level of output, plus a random, unpredictable shock, ϵ_t, which neither the policy authorities nor the public can predict. The portion of the money stock based on last period's output $(\alpha_1 y_{t-1})$ is known to the public and can be thought of as feedback policy because it depends on past values of observed variables. The invariance proposition states that the parameter α_1 of the feedback rule that is set by the authorities has no effect on the behavior of output in the economy. Only the unanticipated part of the money stock (ϵ_t) will cause output to deviate from its full-employment level.

The nature of this result can be illustrated in Figure 2.3. Suppose that the public expects the money authorities to increase the money stock from period $t - 1$ to period t, which implies that the aggregate demand curve will shift from AD^0 to AD^1.

Rational actors will not expect the price level to remain at P_0. Suppose they guess that the price level will shift up the same initial amount that the money stock increased, that is, the vertical distance from AD^0 to AD^1. Then, as they change their price expectations, the aggregate supply curve will shift from AS^0 to AS^1. In fact, the actual price level will, in the absence of any shocks, be P_1. The public's expectations will turn out to be correct. Output remains at y_p while prices rise by the same amount as the money stock is expected to rise. Thus anticipated increases in the money stock will have no effect on output but will only affect prices.

With rational expectations, the price expectations are determined within the model in light of future developments of the money supply. This can be expressed as

$$_{t-1}P_t^\epsilon = E(P_t \mid I_{t-1}) \qquad \text{rational expectations} \qquad (2.4)$$

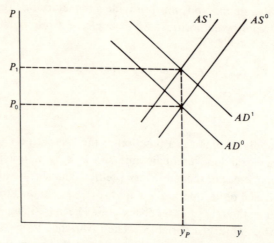

Figure 2.3   An anticipated increase in the money supply.

This equation asserts that people's subjective, psychological expectation of the price level $(_{t-1}P_t^\epsilon)$ equals the *mathematical expectation* of the price level, given both the structure of the model and the information available. In a sense this equation makes the expectation of prices an *endogenous* variable in the model, a variable determined within the system as opposed to being determined outside the model.

An analysis of the model [equations (2.1) to (2.4)] can provide further insights into the nature of the invariance proposition. Using the aggregate demand and supply equations (2.1 and 2.2), y_t can be eliminated, yielding

$$M_t + \bar{V} - P_t = y_p + \beta(P_t - {_{t-1}}P_t^\epsilon) \qquad (2.5)$$

Taking the mathematical expectation of both sides of the equation as of time $t - 1$ gives

$$\alpha_1 y_{t-1} + \bar{V} - {_{t-1}}P_t^\epsilon = y_p \qquad (2.6)$$

or

$$_{t-1}P_t^\epsilon = \alpha_1 y_{t-1} + \bar{V} - y_p \qquad (2.6')$$

In the derivation of equation (2.6') three basic points should be emphasized. (1) The expected money ($\alpha_1 y_{t-1}$) was determined via the money supply rule. The public knows that, in fact, the money stock will differ from what they expect by ϵ_t, but at time $t - 1$, their best guess of ϵ_t is zero. (2) The rational expectations hypothesis is invoked when the mathematical expectation of the price, $E[P_t \mid I_{t-1}]$, is equated with the public's psychological expectation $_{t-1}P_t^\epsilon$. (3) The expected forecast error $E(P_t - _{t-1}P_t^\epsilon \mid I_{t-1})$ is zero, reflecting the fact that, on average, the rational public is correct in its forecast. If the public behaved in such a way as to produce a systematic error in predicting the price level, they would not be making rational forecasts. A rational forecast, by definition, has the property that the expected error is zero.

We can now solve for the price, P_t, by substituting equation (2.6′) into equation (2.5). Simplifying gives the expression

$$P_t = \alpha y_{t-1} + \bar{V} - y_p + \frac{\epsilon_t}{1 + \beta} \qquad (2.7)$$

Therefore the gap between the actual price and the expected price is

$$P_t - _{t-1}P_t^\epsilon = \frac{\epsilon_t}{1 + \beta} \qquad (2.8)$$

Using the Lucas supply equation, we find that output will equal

$$y_t = y_p + \frac{\beta}{1 + \beta} (\epsilon_t) \qquad (2.9)$$

This equation for output reflects the invariance proposition. Only the unanticipated part of the money supply (ϵ_t) affects output. The predictable part of the money supply affects prices but not the level of output. Thus output fluctuates randomly around the full-employment level, with the fluctuations due to unanticipated movements in the money stock. The behavior of output, therefore, is independent of any predictable countercyclical (or even procyclical) policy by the monetary authorities. Any predictable rule for monetary policy is as good as any other from the viewpoint of output determination. The behavior of prices will, however, reflect the choice of the feedback rule.

There are several key elements that drive this analysis. The first key feature is the *neutrality* of anticipated money in the model. That is, an anticipated change in the stock of money will only affect nominal magnitudes (prices) but not real variables such as output. In turn, anticipated changes in prices do not affect any real variables. The second key feature is the Lucas supply equation: Prices are fully flexible and output deviates from full employment only when prices differ from their anticipated levels. In the absence of any surprise in the price level the economy will remain at the full-employment level. The final element in the analysis concerns the information that is available to individual producers. In these simple models individuals are assumed to possess local information rather than any economy-wide or global information.

Relaxing any of these key assumptions will, in general, weaken the strong invariance results. Therefore it is useful to examine briefly each of these key elements of the model.

Neutrality

Neutrality propositions have a long history in monetary theory, and many of the issues are summarized in Don Patinkin's (1965) classic book, *Money, Interest and Prices*. One potential source of nonneutrality is government debt. In a world in which there is outstanding government debt in nominal units of account, money will be neutral *if and only if* the public recognizes that the outstanding bonds will require tax payments to service the interest on the bonds and the public fully discounts these tax payments in its calculation of net worth. To see the logic of this point, suppose the public did not take into account these tax payments and thereby treated the government bonds as an asset of the private sector. An increase in the price level would lower the value of these bonds, the public would then feel their net worth was reduced, and its behavior would be affected. If the future tax payments were taken fully into account, the public would recognize that the lower real value of interest payments would translate into lower real taxes and there would be no change in net worth, and hence, in behavior. The degree to which the private sector recognizes that interest payments on government bonds will necessitate higher taxes, and the degree to which the future taxes are discounted, therefore, plays an important role in the neutrality of money. Unless future tax payments are discounted *fully*, money will not be neutral.

This is a very strong assumption. Many households anticipate higher incomes in the future and would like to borrow against higher expected future income to boost current consumption. Banks usually are not willing to make loans of this nature, and households are *constrained* in this market for loans. Because they are constrained, the effective discount rate for future income is higher than the prevailing interest rate that they can earn on savings. Thus future tax payments are discounted at a *higher* rate than the interest rate is, and in these circumstances, an increase in public debt will increase private wealth. The key issue is the degree to which households are truly constrained in the market for loans.

A more recent issue in monetary theory has been the "superneutrality" of money; that is, whether the *rate of growth* of the money stock can have, even in the long run, an effect on real variables. In the original money growth models, such as Tobin's (1965), the rate of growth of money did affect capital formation. Higher rates of money growth lead to higher inflation rates, causing a portfolio substitution as investors shift away from money and into real capital. In the long run a higher money growth rate would lead to a higher steady-state capital stock. Miguel Sidrauski (1967) developed money growth models based on individual optimizing behavior, in which the long-run capital stock was *not* affected by the rate of monetary expansion. Sidrauski showed that the steady-state capital stock was determined by a modified golden rule and was independent of the rate of monetary expansion. More recently Stanley Fischer (1979) has shown that even in the Sidrauski model the rate of capital accumulation on the approach to the steady state is affected by the rate of monetary expansion, even though the steady-state capital stock is invariant to the money growth rate. Thus the rate of monetary expansion is likely to have an effect on real variables apart from any effects arising from expectational errors.

Features of the institutional environment also play an important role in the neutrality of money. Market "imperfections," such as interest rate ceilings and regulations, serve to diminish the likelihood of the neutrality of money. Perhaps the tax laws that are written in nominal terms are more important. In recent years the interaction between inflation and taxes has been studied quite intensively. Inflation, whether or not anticipated, does matter for the income tax, the tax treatment of capital gains, and the tax treatment of depreciation.

The conclusion to be drawn from this brief survey of the literature is to indicate that, on purely theoretical grounds, one should not expect complete neutrality. Coupled with some obvious institutional features of the tax system, it is very unlikely that, in practice, money is completely neutral. The invariance propositions must, therefore, be taken as approximations. Advocates of these propositions must argue that the nonneutralities are small enough so as not to dominate the basic empirical proposition that only unanticipated money growth affects real variables. To be fair, little evidence has been presented that places these nonneutralities at the center of business cycle developments. In other words, although they may affect the level of output, there is little reason to suspect that nonneutralities cause fluctuations in output.

The specification of aggregate supply

The second basis for the invariance propositions is the hypothesis that prices are flexible and output only deviates from capacity when current prices deviate from expected prices. This proposition (the Lucas supply function) can be challenged from many perspectives. The most obvious and crude alternative perspective is textbook Keynesianism, in which prices are simply fixed and changes in the money stock, whether or not anticipated, have a direct impact on output. This is true, for example, in the familiar IS-LM model. However, wage and price behavior is admittedly nonrational in this model. A more interesting theoretical question is whether it is possible, within rational expectation models, for the anticipated part of the money stock to affect the probability distribution of real output and other real variables. This theoretical strategy accepts the rational expectation framework but examines the consequences of ''rational'' price or wage rigidity.

Phelps and Taylor (1977) and Fischer (1977a) have developed models in which there is rational wage or price setting. In Fischer's model, for example, wage contracts are set two periods in advance. Agents know the monetary policy rule, the structure of the model, and the type of uncertainty in the environment when making their nominal wage commitments. Fischer shows that the choice of the parameters of the monetary policy rule does make a difference. The monetary authorities cannot affect the average or mean level of output but can affect the variability of output around trend. How can this be done? The answer hinges on the nature of the labor contract. When a worker makes his two-period commitment, he knows that the authorities will be able to react to disturbances *before* his two-period wage commitment terminates. Entering into the contract, the worker adjusts his wage in each period based on the *expected* disturbances but still recognizes that the authorities will react in a predictable way to future demand and supply shocks. Because the authorities will be free to counteract the disturbance while workers must stick to their nominal contracts, there is room for policy rules to affect output. In particular, if the authority wishes to increase the level of output in the face of an adverse supply shock that lowers output, they can announce that they will respond to adverse supply shocks by increasing the money stock. This will have the effect of increasing prices and lowering the real wage of the workers in the second period of their two-period nominal contract. With lower real wages, employers will hire more labor, produce more output, and thereby offset the original disturbance. Thus neutralizing an adverse supply shock requires higher prices.

Workers know the policy rules of the authorities and therefore recognize that their second period real wage may be altered in the face of new information received by the authorities. It is important to realize that the authorities cannot affect the average level of output by a policy of systematically increasing the money supply in the second period of the contracts. The reason is that workers would soon recognize such a policy and adjust their money wages for their second period of the contract accordingly. Thus the authorities may be able to affect the variability of output or employment but cannot affect its mean or average level.

Models of this type can be adopted for policy use. Taylor (1979) estimated a model along similar lines and illustrated a mechanism for calculating optimal monetary policy. As Taylor indicated, the trade-offs that face policymakers in these models are quite different from those we are normally accustomed to. In this kind of model, there are trade-offs between the *variability* of output and the variability of the inflation rate. For example, in the presence of an adverse supply shock, prices will rise but output will fall. A policy to stabilize output will require, as we have seen, a *higher* price level. The policymakers must decide whether they wish to have more variability in prices in order to stabilize output. The average level of output in these models is the full-employment level, whereas the average inflation rate is determined by the average rate of money growth. There are no trade-offs involved in the choice of an average inflation rate. Trade-offs only arise regarding the choice of variability in the inflation rate versus variability of output.

These models, in which the invariance propositions do not hold, have had their critics. The main focus of the criticism has been the essential feature of the models, the nominal contracts themselves. The question the critics pose is simple: Why should rational economic actors enter into contracts in which the nominal wage is fixed in advance? By setting their nominal wage in advance, the workers are giving the authorities a chance to stabilize the economy by *destabilizing* their real wages.

Barro (1977b) argues that the type of wage contracts used in Fischer's model are inconsistent with rational behavior. He suggests that Pareto-efficient labor contracts would determine employment independently of any perceived monetary disturbances. If this were not the case there would be room for mutually advantageous gains from trade. In Fischer's model, workers and firms negotiate contracts that may lead to divergences between the marginal product of labor and the marginal value of time during the second period of the contract. Barro questions whether workers and firms would actually write contracts that permitted inefficiencies of this sort.

Fischer (1977b) admits that he has no deep justification for the form of the contract but appeals to the evidence that labor contracts do, in practice, take a form similar to those in this model. He also argues that Barro neglects one important fact: Drawing up and monitoring contracts can be expensive. If there were no costs in distinguishing between changes in the average price level and changes in relative prices, then Barro's argument would be compelling. In a world without any costs of distinguishing between these two distinct events, employment would not be affected by pure changes in the price level but would, most likely, be affected by relative changes in other input prices. Fischer argues that, in practice, it is impossible to disentangle these events so that contracts dictating different responses to the two events would be impossible to enforce and administer. If there were no costs of observing the true state of affairs, contracts would be written to reflect every possible contingency. This is, in fact, what the very abstract Arrow–Debreu model of general equilibrium does, but "costs" of some type prevent all these contingency markets from existing.

An example may be useful here. Suppose a foreign cartel raised the price of its product, say, oil. Firms might argue that in this situation they could only pay lower wages as their materials costs have risen. They, therefore, might want to cut workers' money wages. On the other hand, workers might view the oil price increase as part of a spell of temporary inflation and want their nominal wage rates increased. It would be almost impossible to imagine writing a contract ex ante for this event as well as difficult to obtain agreement ex post.

If there were no costs involved in writing, monitoring, or enforcing contracts, then Barro's argument would be persuasive. Fischer argues that because there are real costs involved, it is uncertain whether contracts fixing the nominal wage may, in fact, be all that bad. These issues are complex and some progress has been made by Blanchard (1979) and Hall and Lilien (1979) in outlining models of contracts in which costs may be important. For example, Blanchard considers the behavior of the economy under alternative indexing rules when there are costs of including more accurate information into the indexing rules. Hall and Lilien argue that a system under which employers unilaterally decide on layoffs but must pay steep overtime premiums to workers may approximate a world in which firms and workers are achieving an efficient allocation of labor in the presence of shocks. An uneasy tension between conformity with traditional canons of rational behavior and a desire to explain concrete labor market phenomena pervades this literature and, most likely, will continue to do so for some time still.

This debate about contracts is also related to disputes concerning the interpretation of layoffs. In Barro's vision, "layoffs" would only occur when the marginal value of leisure time exceeded the perceived marginal product or shadow price of labor. In the absence of distorting taxes or subsidies these layoffs would be efficient. In Fischer's model, and certainly in the traditional Keynesian model, layoffs are not subtle indicators of the shadow price of leisure time but are indications of inefficiencies.

In a series of papers McCallum (1977, 1980) argued that some types of price stickiness were compatible with the invariance propositions. McCallum essentially developed models in which prices were independent of current demand conditions but were set in the previous period in anticipation of the current period money stock. Frydman (1981), however, demonstrated that McCallum's models of price stickiness implied unreasonable behavior for inventories and thus were not very plausible.

In summary, the invariance proposition requires that when contracts are present, markets must work essentially like Arrow–Debreu contingency markets even if, at first glance, they appear to be of a different nature. It would be rather remarkable if economists would agree on the question of whether or not markets mimicked the Arrow–Debreu world or, in other words, whether existing market institutions really act like "perfect" markets in all respects.

The information structure

The invariance propositions depend intimately on the information structure built into the economic models. Most of the early models in the literature limited individuals' access to contemporaneous information to prices in local markets. However, even in simple macro models it seems plausible to make *some* global information available to economic agents, especially financial market information such as an economy-wide interest rate. McCallum (1980) demonstrated that including an economy-wide interest rate in individuals' information sets can invalidate the invariance proposition – that is, parameters of a money supply feedback rule can affect the probability distribution of real output. The current period interest rate conveys information to economic agents about the unknown disturbances impinging on the economy and this information will, in general, be influenced by the policy rule employed. This is not a completely general result, as Barro (1980a) has constructed a model that includes an economy-wide interest rate and yet the invariance proposition remains intact. However, as McCallum (1980) stresses, the invariance propositions are extremely sensitive to the information structure built into the models and the precise specification of the underlying equations.

Two other studies illustrate this basic point. Weiss (1980) constructed a model in which one group of economic actors (capitalists) had access to some information concerning the future profitability of investment while another group (workers) did not. This information about the future profitability of investment was a determinant of the current price level. Because the workers only had access to local information and lacked knowledge of the future profitability of investment, they would misperceive the current price level. Workers would, therefore, be unable to make the link between movements in their nominal wages and movements in their real wages. Weiss showed that an activist monetary policy could alleviate this problem and thereby prevent the workers from misperceiving the current price level. A monetary rule that responded to productivity shocks as they occurred could neutralize the influence of future productivity shocks on the current price level. Thus Weiss effectively demonstrated that in the presence of asymmetric information the form of the monetary policy rule could play an important role in stabilizing output.

King (1981) explored the possibility of incorporating a currently observed monetary aggregate in agents' information sets in a rational expectations model. If the agents could observe the monetary aggregate perfectly, there obviously would be no relation between money and output because there would be no possibility for changes in the money stock to "fool" agents. King examined the consequences of allowing agents to observe the contemporaneous money stock subject to some error, that is, a "noisy" money stock. His principal finding was that there should be no significant relation between movements in output and movements in the contemporaneously perceived money stock. This means that if an econometrician had the same information as individuals, he should also find no correlation between money and output. It is evident that changes in the information set can radically change the properties of these models.

Although these results suggest that the invariance proposition is not likely to be strictly true, they do not suggest that stabilization policy can be successfully conducted in the same manner that was appropriate for the traditional Keynesian models. Agents in these newer models have rational expectations and therefore take into account proposed policy stances–policy rules must be formulated in this light. In addition, economic policy can at best only affect the variance of output but cannot affect its mean value. Although there may be some scope for policy even in the flexible price versions of the rational expectations models, the nature of the policy problem is fundamentally changed.

The question of persistence

Early critics of equilibrium business cycles theories contended that these theories could not explain the duration or persistence of the typical business cycle. For example, Franco Modigliani (1977:5) argued:

> [in these theories] errors of price expectations, which are the only source of departure from the natural state, cannot be avoided, but they can only be short-lived and random. In particular, there cannot be persistent unemployment above the natural rate for this would imply high serial correlation between the successive errors of expectations, which is inconsistent with rational expectations.

To clarify Modigliani's position, we should recall the expression derived for equilibrium output:

$$y_t = y_p + \frac{\beta}{1 + \beta} (\epsilon_t) \tag{2.9}$$

Deviations of output from full employment only occur because of the random, unpredictable shocks to the money supply, ϵ_t.

The only shocks to the system are mistakes in predicting the money stock. The orthogonality property of conditional expectations requires that they be uncorrelated over time; that is, knowledge of past mistakes should contain no predictive power for future mistakes. This implies that the correlation between successive levels of output will also be zero. Because the only source of a deviation from full employment is these random forecast errors, the levels of output must also be uncorrelated.

Practically, this means that if output is greater than full employment this period, there is no reason whatsoever to predict that the next period's output will be anything but full employment. A positive ϵ_t this period contains no information about ϵ_{t+1}; the best guess for the next period's disturbance is still zero, and thus the best guess for the next period's level of output is full employment. Unfortunately, this implication of the theory is strongly rejected by the data. If the economy is in a boom this period, most likely it will continue next period and, conversely, for recessions. In other words, movements of output, employment, and unemployment all tend to *persist*. If they exceed their trend or normal levels in a given period, these variables tend to remain above trend.

It is clear that our rational expectations model must be modified in some manner to be consistent with the data – otherwise, Modigliani's criticism would be fatal. Proponents of rational expectation models do not, of course, deny that output and employment series are correlated over time. Instead, they suggest simple modifications of equilibrium models that make them more realistic and capable of explaining the persistence that is observed. There are two basic ways to construct rational expectations models that explain the persistence of the business cycle. If individuals do not become aware of their forecast errors until several periods later, then their forecast errors can be correlated. Individuals have no way of knowing that their mistakes are, in fact, related, and therefore have no way to correct this systematic error. Lucas (1975) has constructed a model that has this feature. The second type of rational expectation model that can explain persistence has the random shocks causing the level of potential output to vary over the business cycle. The reason that potential or "full-employment" output can vary is that the random shocks affect the stock of inventories or other types of capital and with different levels of inventories or capital stocks, the level of full employment will vary.

Alan Blinder and Stanley Fischer (1981) presented a clear model that links uncorrelated forecast errors to persistent movements of output. The central mechanism by which this is accomplished in their model is through the stock of inventories. An unanticipated increase in the money stock will cause an unanticipated rise in the price level. The firm, perceiving that part of its price change may be a change in its relative price, will increase production and also run down its inventory stock. In the short run output will increase and the stock of inventories will fall. Once the firm has recognized that it was fooled by the aggregate price increase, it will wish to resume normal production, except that its stock of inventories is below its desired levels. The firm must, therefore, produce above its normal level until inventory stocks are restored to desired levels. The initial mistake in predicting inflation can lead to a long period when output is above "normal." In other words, the stock of inventories affects the level of normal or full-employment output.

Blinder and Fischer essentially modify the aggregate supply curve. Letting N_t represent the stock of inventories and N^* the desired stock of inventories, they modify the aggregate supply relation to read:

$$y_t = \alpha(N^* - N_t) + \beta(P_t - {}_{t-1}P_t^\epsilon) \qquad (2.10)$$

Even if the private sector perfectly predicts the price level, output will be above trend if inventories are below their desired levels. A price surprise that induces firms to sell out of their inventories will, therefore, lead to persistent movements in output.

Another possible mechanism for explaining fluctuations in potential output is changes in investment, and hence the capital stock that can occur when agents are fooled by aggregate price movements. If changes in prices are perceived to be both real and permanent, then agents may wish to undertake some investments. Unanticipated movements in the aggregate price level will, in part, be perceived in this way, depending, of course, on the agents' past experience with price signals. An economy-wide investment boom will lead to increases in output by the traditional "accelerator" effects but will also leave the economy with a capital stock that is *higher* than the level that would have been desired in the presence of full information. We would expect, therefore, subsequent capital accumulation to be less than usual, following the price surprise. Unlike the case of inventories, a price surprise should cause output to be initially higher than usual from the accelerator mechanism but then fall below its normal value as firms slow down their investment rate to decrease their capital stock.

Inventories and capital formation do not exhaust the mechanisms whereby initial random shocks can give rise to persistent output movements. Sargent (1979) showed that in the presence of adjustment costs for changing its stock of labor, a firm will have a dynamic labor demand schedule that depends on the last period's level of employment. Combined with a dynamic labor supply schedule, this can give rise to serially correlated movements of real wage and employment.

Adjustment costs, capital accumulation, and inventories can explain why output and employment can exhibit persistence, but why should the *unemployment* rate behave in a similar fashion? There are two possible explanations for the persistence of unemployment. First, one can argue, as Lucas does, that the unemployment rate merely reflects the level of wages currently available in the economy. If wages are below normal for several periods, respondents to the unemployment survey may report that they are looking for jobs at their normal wage. Thus persistence in the unemployment rate may simply mirror persistence in real wage movements.

An alternative explanation rests with search theory. Optimal search policy for a job can often be characterized by a reservation-wage policy; that is, there exists a wage rate known as the reservation wage such that an offer is only accepted if it exceeds the reservation wage. If a person is searching for a job and follows the reservation-wage rule, there is a certain probability that he will not find a job in any given period and will continue to search for one. This implies that a fraction of the unemployment pool will remain unemployed, which can account for some persistence in the unemployment rate.

These explanations for the persistence of unemployment are not so persuasive as the explanations for the persistence of output or employment. Critics argue that a much simpler explanation for the persistence in unemployment is that in a recession jobs are scarce and recessions tend to persist. Of course, this is the same dispute we discussed earlier in this chapter concerning the interpretation of unemployment. Is unemployment essentially a phenomenon of choice (even though the choice set may be poor) or is it an indication of disequilibrium? Accepting the accounts of persistence consistent with rational expectations models precludes a simple disequilibrium interpretation of unemployment.

We have seen that Modigliani's early criticism of rational expectations models is only true for simple versions of the theory, and extensions of the basic model can account for the "persistence" problem. As Lucas and Sargent (1978:66) write, "Even though the new classical theory implies that forecast errors which are the aggregate demand 'impulses' are serially uncorrelated, it is certainly logically possible that 'propagation mechanisms' are at work that convert these impulses into serially correlated movements in real variables like output and employment." As a logical proposition, Lucas and Sargent are certainly correct; the real question is whether these theories, in fact, account for observed behavior.

What is the evidence?

There have been many empirical studies in the recent past on the topic of rational expectations and aggregate supply. What will be attempted here is to highlight the main thrust of the empirical work by focusing on a few studies. The two basic questions that we will examine are

1. Does the Lucas aggregate supply function allow us, in practice, to explain business fluctuations? and
2. What evidence is there for the invariance proposition; that is, is it true that anticipated money growth has no effect on real variables?

The first piece of evidence concerning the Lucas supply function focuses on the difference between countries with very volatile inflation rates and those with stable inflation rates. Recall from the earlier discussion that unanticipated inflation will have a greater effect on production decisions when the environment is characterized by low aggregate price volatility. In that case unanticipated inflation will be perceived by individuals to be relative price movements and production decisions will change. If the price level is very volatile, economic actors will largely discount movements in prices, attributing them to general inflation and thus not alter production rates.

Lucas (1973) tested this idea by examining the relationship between inflation volatility and output movements across countries. He constructed rational expectation models linking the volatility of aggregate demand for goods and services to the volatility of prices and finally to the responsiveness of suppliers to changes in demand. In his model a country that had a volatile demand management policy attributable to erratic money growth rates would have a volatile aggregate price level and producers would not be very responsive to changes in aggregate demand. Countries with stable demand policies would have more predictable price levels and producers would be less responsive to changes in aggregate demand.

Lucas estimated models for a spectrum of countries. In countries with very volatile aggregate demand, producers respond very little to changes in demand, whereas the responsiveness is much higher in countries with more stable demand policies. This can be seen in Table 2.1, which presents Lucas's data for several countries, by comparing the United States and Argentina. The variance in aggregate demand is about twenty-five times greater in Argentina than in the United States, whereas the "responsiveness coefficient" is 0.910

Table 2.1. *Lucas's cross-country evidence*

	π	var ΔP_t	var ΔX_t
Argentina	0.011	0.01998	0.01555
Canada	0.759	0.00018	0.00139
West Germany	0.820	0.00026	0.00073
Italy	0.622	0.00044	0.00040
U.S.A.	0.910	0.00007	0.00064

Note: π = measure of responsiveness of output to the growth in nominal demand; var ΔX_t = variance in the growth rate of nominal demand; var ΔP_t = variance of the inflation rate.
Source: Tables I and II, Lucas (1973).

in the United States but only 0.011 in Argentina. Table 2.1 also indicates that within the group of countries with more moderate experiences the evidence on volatility and responsiveness is somewhat mixed. For example, Italy had a less volatile measure of aggregate demand than either West Germany or Canada, but Italy's responsiveness was less than the other two countries'. Thus the evidence is only persuasive for the extreme cases and says little about countries with only slightly dissimilar inflation experiences. In their reexamination of Lucas's model, Froyen and Waud (1980) find a similar result – there was only a very weak connection between the volatility of aggregate demand and the slope of the short-run inflation–output relationship.

Many studies have taken a time-series approach to our two basic questions. Barro (1977a) provided some initial evidence that indicated that the rational expectations hypothesis could not be dismissed simply as a theoretical curiosum. His approach was to use past values for money growth and other lagged variables to forecast money growth. These forecast equations were then identified explicitly with agents' expectations of money growth rates. In other words, Barro assumed that economic actors in the economy acted *as if* they used regression analysis on readily available data to forecast money growth rates. The forecast errors from the regressions predicting money growth were termed "unanticipated money growth" and used to test the hypothesis that fluctuations in unemployment around the natural rate depended only on *unanticipated* money growth. The natural rate of unemployment was allowed to be affected by variables reflecting minimum wage laws and the draft. Barro tested his hypothesis by entering the actual money growth rates into the equation to determine if they added significant explanatory power to the regression explaining unemployment in terms of unanticipated money growth. Because they did not, Barro argued that he could not reject the hypothesis that *only* unanticipated money growth causes unemployment to deviate from its natural rate.

Barro's work has not been free of criticism. One key difficulty of any work of this nature is the identification of forecast equations for money growth with agents' actual expectations. If other information is readily available, rational agents should incorporate it into their forecasts. In particular, Small (1979) argued that information concerning the budgetary aspects of the Vietnam War was available to agents, and they should have anticipated higher money growth rates than Barro's equations predicted. Controlling for this factor and also modifying Barro's measure of the draft variable led Small to conclude that Barro's evidence on the invariance proposition was quite weak. Although Barro (1979), in turn, criticized some aspects of Small's work, their controversy illustrates the difficulty of ascertaining exactly what a "rational" agent should know.

There are other studies using similar methodologies that basically support Barro's findings. For example, J. Grossman (1979) used nominal Gross National Product (GNP) as a proxy for policy instruments to test the hypothesis that only unanticipated movements in nominal income cause fluctuations in unemployment from its natural rate. Grossman's study used quarterly data as contrasted to Barro's original study on annual data. He also claimed to find support for the invariance proposition.

The "successful" tests of the invariance proposition do contain an important and unexplained element. Taking Grossman's study as an example, we see that his equation relating unemployment to unanticipated nominal demand has the form

$$UN_t = 1.39 \cdot UN_{t-1} - 0.434 \cdot UN_{t-2} \qquad (2.11)$$
$$+ \sum_{j=0}^{5} k_j \, UDY_{t-j} + C$$

where

UN_t = the unemployment rate at time t

UDY_{t-j} = unanticipated nominal income growth at time $t - j$

k_j = coefficients on unanticipated nominal income

C = constant

This equation explains movements in unemployment in terms of lagged unemployment and unanticipated nominal income growth. According to the rational expectations hypothesis, surprises in nominal income (the variable being forecasted) should be random, so that we can rewrite this equation as

$$UN_t = 1.39 \cdot UN_{t-1} - 0.434 \, UN_{t-2}$$
$$+ \text{ random surprises } + C \qquad (2.12)$$

The unemployment equation contains two lagged unemployment terms and implies that a random surprise in nominal income will cause the unemployment rate to deviate from its long-run rate and then oscillate around this rate until it returns finally to long-run equilibrium. This means that for several quarters after the shock the unemployment rate will still be away from its long-run value as it follows a path returning to equilibrium. At every point in time during this transition period the unemployment rate reflects equilibrium in the labor market, and hence we can say that the unemployment rate is at the "natural rate" at all times following the initial surprise. The natural rate of unemployment, in these models, is not a constant or a slow-moving variable at all; it exhibits cyclical behavior just like other macroeconomic variables. What this means is that the full-employment unemployment rate varies rather sharply over the business cycle and that most fluctuations in the unemployment rate reflect *movements of the natural rate* rather than *deviations of unemployment from the natural rate*. In other words, the level of full employment moves with the business cycle. Why should this occur?

We can put this issue into broader perspective. The essential point is whether shocks to the system can systematically affect the natural rate of output or the natural rate of unemployment so that the persistence of the business cycle can be explained. As discussed earlier, there is, in principle, an explanation for these persistence effects. In practice, however, lagged unemployment and output terms are simply added to the regressions to pick up the obvious serial correlation in the time series without any deep theoretical justification. There has been little empirical work done to date to account explicitly for the importance of the lagged terms in unemployment and output. This is a serious weakness with the evidence thus far produced, perhaps even more serious than the lack of a perfect expectation proxy. One exception to this general point is Sargent's (1978) empirical study of dynamic labor demand.

Mishkin (1982) has questioned the received evidence in support of the invariance proposition on the grounds that it fails to test separately for the two key elements that drive the theory: the rationality of expectations and the neutrality of money. Barro's work assumed that agents' forecasts were based on true regressions of money growth on past variables; Mishkin maintained that this assumption can and should be tested. He also showed that it was possible to test the neutrality assumption in conjunction with the rationality hypothesis.

Mishkin's procedure is straightforward. A general aggregate supply relationship that allows for both anticipated money growth (M^a) and unanticipated money growth ($M - M^a$) can be written as

$$y_t = \sum_{i=0}^{n} a_i(M_{t-i} - M_{t-i}^a) + \sum_{j=0}^{n} b_j (M_{t-j}^a) + \epsilon_t \quad (2.13)$$

$$M^a = \beta X_t \quad (2.14)$$

Let X_t be a vector of variables available at $t - 1$ that help predict money growth at time t,

Substituting (2.14) into (2.13) yields

$$y_t = \sum_{i=0}^{n} a_i(M_{t-i} - \beta X_{t-i}) + \sum_{j=0}^{n} b_j (\beta X_{t-j}) + \epsilon_t \quad (2.15)$$

As Mishkin notes, equations (2.14) and (2.15) can be estimated jointly and it is possible to test whether the estimated value for ''β'' in equation (2.14) is the same as the estimated value for β in equation (2.15). This test, based on the overidentifying restrictions in the model, is a test for rational expectations. It tests whether the expectations of money growth *implicit* in the aggregate supply curve are consistent with the actual processes governing money growth. If the statistical tests indicate that the values for β calculated in both equations are statistically different, then expectational rationality can be rejected.

It is also possible to test whether anticipated money growth has an effect by testing the hypothesis that the b_j are equal to zero. Mishkin's own empirical results somewhat support the assumption of rational expectations but generally throw doubt on the neutrality of money assumption. In addition, Mishkin also found that when the lag length was increased in Barro's model, tests of the invariance proposition no longer support the hypothesis.

Both Mishkin's and Barro's work are reduced form approaches to economic fluctuations. That is, they link anticipated and unanticipated money growth that are taken to be exogenous variables to the levels of output and unemployment that are endogenous variables. Although reduced form studies are certainly useful, they raise as many questions as they answer. For example, in Mishkin's model, anticipated money growth first increases output for several quarters but then depresses output back to the normal level. Why should output be related to anticipated money growth in this way? Does it reflect the structure of labor contracts, industrial pricing agreements, capital formation, or features of the tax system? Reduced form studies are silent on these important questions.

Gordon (1981) has forcefully challenged the studies claiming to find support for the invariance proposition. According to Gordon, these studies have not specified a clear alternative hypothesis to confront the invariance proposition. Most macroeconomists agree that money is neutral in the long run so that the only remaining issue is the short-run neutrality of anticipated money. Gordon developed a model of gradual price adjustment, which included the models leading to the invariance proposition as special cases. Money is neutral in Gordon's alternative model in the long run, but anticipated money growth may be nonneutral in the short run.

Gordon's empirical work on quarterly data covered the period 1890–1980. His basic finding was that prices did not move one for one with anticipated changes in nominal income as required by the invariance propositions. This finding was also true for the 1890–1930 period during which prices of commodities were more volatile than in the postwar era. Gordon's work relied on forecasting equations in order to derive a series for anticipated nominal income, and thus his work is subject to the same type of criticism as Barro's in this regard.

Difficulties in evaluating all this econometric work are compounded by the *identification problem* first raised by Sargent (1976). The identification problem in econometric theory refers to the problem of inferring the structure of a system from information about the reduced form. The classic example of an identification problem arises in demand and supply analysis. From price and quantity data alone it is impossible to determine either the supply or demand curve. Because equilibrium prices and quantities must lie along both curves, additional information about the system is needed to estimate the separate demand and supply relations.

The particular problem that arises in the aggregate supply literature concerns the inability to discriminate between models for which the invariance proposition holds and those in which it does not. As an example, consider the following extreme "Keynesian" model:

1. Output is determined by a set of variables *excluding* money.
2. The money growth rate is determined by the same set of variables, *plus* the unpredictable change in output. Innovations or surprises in output could affect money growth rates if, for example, the banking system supplied funds at least partially on demand from the private sector.

As Buiter (1980) has shown, this Keynesian model would produce the same reduced form and hence would be *observationally equivalent* to a model in which both anticipated and unanticipated money growth affects output. Although it is possible to make assumptions that ensure identification of the structural model as Buiter (1981) and McCallum (1979) both indicate, the identification problem still clouds the interpretation of the existing empirical work.

It may be useful to summarize the discussion of the evidence into four major points:

1. The proposition that countries with more volatile aggregate demand will exhibit less output responsiveness to inflation holds only for extreme cases.
2. Several studies now exist that purport to show that only certain *unanticipated* variables affect real variables such as output and unemployment. More recent work, however, casts doubt on these results, particularly when they are examined in the context of more general models.
3. Existing *empirical* work fails to justify the persistence effects that are so important in the studies.
4. Identification problems add to the difficulties of interpreting the empirical work.

The jury is still out on the question of which type of rational expectation model, if any, provides a useful empirical description of the economy.

The gestalt behind the models

A world in which markets clear and economic actors are farsighted and rational has a distinct pre-Keynesian ring. Keynes's *General Theory*, which set the course for modern macroeconomics, attributed irrational behavior to the private sector. Keynes thought that workers tended to confuse real and nominal wages, that stock markets were often just giant betting parlors, and that investment decisions were as often governed by whim and caprice as by purely concrete economic factors. Modern macroeconomics does not subscribe to all of Keynes's notions but does betray a health skepticism to the workings of the market.

James Tobin (1977:461), one of the distinguished pioneers of modern macroeconomics, characterizes the flexible price models of the rational expectation school as, in fact, being nothing but a sophisticated version of pre-Keynesian notions:

> They are all inspired by faith that the economy can never be very far from equilibrium. Markets work, excess supplies and demand are eliminated, expectations embody the best available information, people always make any and all deals which would move all parties to preferred positions. With such faith the orthodox economists of the early 1930's could shut their eyes to events they knew *a priori* could not be happening
> . . . Keynes might say this is where he came in.

Rather than denying this, some rational expectation theorists, for example, Robert Lucas and Thomas Sargent, call themselves modern classical economists.

What is at stake are two radically distinct visions or descriptions of prices and markets and their functioning in the economy. A rough characterization of the Keynesian position due to Tobin might be as follows. In modern capitalist economies markets respond slowly to excess demand and supply, particularly to excess supply. This makes the economy susceptible to prolonged periods of unemployment and excess capacity. Investment decisions are often governed by intangible factors such as the state of long-term expectations about the health and climate for business. Even if markets were very flexible, price adjustments may in fact be destabilizing. Price adjustments that are too rapid may create uncertainty and unsettling business conditions.

This last point deserves elaboration. Keynes devoted Chapter 19 of the *General Theory* to this essential question: Would freely flexible wages and prices, in fact, be desirable? After surveying all the potential channels by which falling wages and prices could restore an economy back to full employment, Keynes concluded that the falling wages would, on balance, have adverse effects. During a period of falling wages firms might continue to postpone investment in search of the elusive time when wage levels would reach their minimum. Falling wages and prices would cause bankruptcies, labor unrest, and unsettling business conditions. On net, Keynes concluded, a stable wage level should be the goal of public policy. There is a deep distrust of the flexible price world running through the *General Theory*.

Current discussions of economic policy often stress the malfunctioning of markets. Wages are frequently said to rise because of union power and prices are allegedly pushed up by firms with substantial market power. Union settlements are claimed to be governed by what rival unions gain and not by fundamental considerations of cost and demand. From these beliefs come cries for wage and price controls or clever tax schemes to slow the growth of wage inflation.

The alternative vision of the flexible price models of the rational expectations school is close to Tobin's characterization of pre-Keynesian economists. Markets are viewed as sensitive barometers and indicators of current and future developments and are efficient processors of information in the economy. Too much is at stake for expectations of future events to be irrational: The profit motive works here as in other areas in the economy. The economy devotes substantial resources to gather information about future occurrences and pays for good forecasting.

The rational expectations vision is buttressed by one simple fact of the modern economy – inflation. In an inflationary environment it becomes more and more difficult to sustain a notion of "wage inflexibility," which is essential to the Keynesian vision. If wages are, in fact, rising at 8 percent per annum, can they really be inflexible? Downward inflexibility in wages in these circumstances means only slower wage growth relative to trend – not the seemingly more painful phenomenon of falling money wages.

As long as wages and prices are set with some view to the future, expectations of the future will play a role in the pricing processes. There may be, as Solow (1980) and Okun (1981) argue, some institutional or even ethical constraints under which the pricing process occurs. But wages and prices do change frequently and, at each price change, the future can be brought into the present. Whether or not this is done with a "rational" or "irrational" view toward the future is a subject of debate, but, at least, in the language of the mystery novel, the motive and opportunity are there for rational actors.

John Taylor (1980) has constructed models of the wage-setting process that combines institutional features of the labor market, such as staggered contracts, with rational expectations. In setting their wage demands, workers look back to recent settlements, look ahead to anticipated ones, and consider the degree to which the authorities are prepared to accommodate the inflationary consequences of wage settlements. Although it may be difficult to determine, in practice, the degree to which wage settlements are backward or forward looking, Taylor shows that as settlements become more forward looking, a disinflation policy will require less sacrifice in terms of unemployment and lost output.

Another possible compromise position between the disparate visions is the "credibility" hypothesis of William Fellner (1979). In Fellner's view, wage and price setters take into account the response of monetary authorities to their decisions. If they believe the money authorities are weak willed, they will push up wages and prices with the knowledge that the monetary authorities will ratify the inflation. A determined and credible monetary authority will deter wage and price increases because the private sector knows that the monetary authorities will not ratify the inflation and unemployment and a recession will follow. Clearly, the expectations of future monetary policy do affect wage and price decisions in this model so that it shares some features of the rational expectations approach. It also shares some features of the alternative views because it allows some scope for the exercise of market power by big firms and unions. The policy advice based on this theory is similar to the policy advice coming from rational expectations models: Set money growth targets to maintain a desired long-run inflation rate and stick to it.

Economists who are somewhat skeptical of the claims of rational expectation models can share in this policy prescription. As long as firms and unions are *somewhat* governed by the anticipated behavior on the part of monetary authorities, then a useful part of a disinflation strategy would be to set money growth targets and stick to them. Although there may be a recession, the recession will be less severe if the monetary authorities are credible. Wage demands will not be so strong if workers believe that the monetary authorities will not ratify their demands.

Of course, the credibility hypothesis is a two-edged sword. If workers and firms know that the political realities will not permit a determined money authority, then inflation will run rampant. Fellner, in this respect, differs sharply from Milton Friedman who denies that monopoly power of any type can cause inflation. In Fellner's world the big actors do have this power, and the monetary authorities need the political will and strength to fight the battle. If the political will and political constellations are not there to back the monetary authorities, then monetary guidelines will be a meaningless exercise. For when the recession comes, the political forces will call for monetary expansion, not restraint.

Testing the credibility hypothesis is a difficult task. It is perhaps even more difficult than testing usual versions of the rational expectations hypothesis because of Fellner's insight that the "monetary rule" is not written on a stone tablet but is a product of political forces. Even defining meaningful expectations of money growth is difficult in this world. Whether formal tests of the model are feasible, some economists will argue for setting goals of money growth and sticking to them. Whether the stated goals would, in practice, bear any resemblance to actual policies is the critical question.

3

Further topics in macroeconomics

One could have easily derived the impression from the last chapter that the sole topic of interest in rational expectations and macroeconomics was the question of aggregate supply or, more broadly, the division of nominal income into inflation and real GNP growth. Although the topic of aggregate supply has been of fundamental interest, the rational expectations revolution has touched on other aspects of macroeconomics. Indeed, the long-run contribution of the ideas from rational expectations may, in fact, be in these other areas rather than on the issues concerning aggregate supply.

In this chapter three important topics will be treated in detail: (1) models in which expectations are rational in some sectors of the economy but not in others; (2) the application of optimal control theory to models in which expectations are formed rationally; and (3) the use of econometric models when agents form expectations rationally. Although each of these issues may seem disjoint from the others, they are united by a common theme – allowing for rational expectations, even in some sectors of the economy, fundamentally changes the use of economic models for explanation, forecasting, and control. A brief introduction to each of these topics is warranted.

A frequently advanced proposition from economists who are critical of flexible price models of aggregate supply is that rational expectation modeling is more appropriate for some sectors of the economy than for others. Generally, financial market efficiency has seemed to these economists to be more plausible than labor or product market efficiency because of the relative ease of arbitraging financial markets. This has led some economists to believe that the "ideal" macroeconomic model would contain rational financial markets but would permit nonrational behavior in some sectors, in particular, in the labor market. William Poole (1976) was one of the first economists to articulate this compromise position. This mixture of models, however, raises some immediate questions. Does the distinction between anticipated and unanticipated money growth remain important? Can changes in the money supply, whether or not anticipated, affect the behavior of output and other real variables? How should policy be conducted in this type of model? In the first section we present a model along these lines with rational financial markets but with a fixed-price Keynesian aggregate supply side. This model, based on Olivier Blanchard's (1981) work, clarifies these issues. Following the analytical presentation, some empirical evidence is presented from econometric models that have been modified along these lines. The evidence, although rather limited, demonstrates that assuming a rational financial sector makes a difference for the dynamic behavior of existing models.

The theory of "optimal control" was one of the glamorous developments in macroeconomics during the 1960s. Optimal control techniques are essentially mathematical devices that allow an economist to find the best possible policy decisions. What is required is an econometric model and a set of preferences over all possible outcomes for the economy. Given these two ingredients, optimal control techniques permit efficient calculation of the best policies. During the 1960s and early 1970s these techniques were refined to handle nonlinear models, models with uncertain coefficients, and even models in which learning about coefficient values was possible. None of these formulations, however, allowed expectations to be formed rationally.

When attempts were made to extend optimal control techniques to rational expectation models, a curious fact was noted. It appeared that optimal policy in some rational expectation model was "inconsistent.'' The term inconsistent in this context has a precise meaning. At time zero policymakers formulated their plans for the policy variables over the whole planning horizon. The performance of the economy was then evaluated assuming that economic agents were aware of the plans of the policymakers. The optimal policy was the plan, known by the economic agents, that gave rise to the best performance for the economy. The inconsistency problem arose because sometime during the actual execution of the plan, poli-cymakers could actually improve welfare by reneging on their original plan and carrying out a new plan. In essence, policymakers had an incentive to cheat, and it appeared that traditional optimal control theory dictated this type of behavior.

The issues involved in this topic are quite complex and only very recently have been understood. In the second section we will try to clarify these issues by a series of examples that illustrate the nature of optimal policy in the presence of rational expectations. The debate has also attracted attention because it seemed to shed light on the perennial question of ''rules versus discretion.'' Our examples will show the connection of this debate to the issues dealing with policy and control.

The final topic, ''Econometric Policy Evaluation,'' is the use of econometric models for policy evaluation when agents are assumed to have rational expectations. The primary figure in the development of this area is, again, Robert E. Lucas. In an important article Lucas demonstrated that econometric models could be seriously misused in evaluation of policy. He indicated that many key equations in econometric models depend rather intimately on the type of policies that are being conducted. Current econometric practice embodies the assumption that the equations of the models do not change when policy changes are contemplated – Lucas showed how this assumption could lead to inaccurate evaluations of the actual consequences of policy changes. In general, when policy changes are made, the very structure of the econometric model will also change and the econ-ometrician neglects this only at his own peril.

Lucas illustrated his point with a series of concrete examples, and we will follow a similar expositional route. It is important to stress that Lucas's criticism of current econometric practice does not rely on special assumptions about unemployment or aggregate supply – it applies to most sectors of a typical econometric model. Almost all modern macroeconomists have had to come to grips with Lucas's criticism, and we will discuss some of the attempts to incorporate these ideas into econometric practice.

Partly rational macro models

Many economists have expressed the belief that financial markets are rational and efficient but that labor markets are not so responsive to new information and have an inertia of their own. Poole wrote:

> The implications of the rational-expectations hypothesis for macro modeling are profound – [and] of greatest importance for the auction markets in financial assets and commodities. These markets embody efficient mechanisms of futures trading and inventory speculation. In the labor market the mechanism forcing consistency between present anticipations and true expected values is weaker; hence, it is possible that neither current nor anticipated near-term market conditions will have much effect on current wages. (1976: 503–4)

Nonrationality in the labor market implies that the whole aggregate supply side of the economy will also be nonrational and that the invariance propositions will not hold.

The alleged rationality of the financial markets still raises interesting questions for macroeconomic theory and policy. Presumably, the latest information about the trends of future policy should then be reflected in the financial markets. Does this mean that changes in government spending or the money stock will have differing consequences depending on whether or not they were anticipated? If anticipations do matter, then the whole dynamic structure of macro models may differ sharply from models in which no sectors exhibit rational behavior. These issues are difficult to treat simply on an a priori basis, and to provide some answers, we should now turn to an explicit model.

The model that we will analyze is adopted from Blanchard (1981) and is essentially a modification of the Hicksian IS-LM model. In pure textbook Keynesian fashion, prices are fixed and the supply of output is determined by aggregate demand for goods and services. This is the simplest and most familiar case of a nonrational aggregate supply sector. The model studied here differs from the IS-LM model in that behavior in the asset markets is assumed to be consistent with rational behavior.

There are three assets in the model: money, very short-term bonds, and equities or stocks. The stock market is rational in a very special sense: Stock prices at any point in time are precisely the present discounted value of future profits in the economy. The model assumes that there is no risk premium for corporate equity. Because the patterns of profits and interest rates over time depend on the behavior of the economy, rational stock market participants must implicitly forecast the whole future path of the economy in order to obtain the current price of stocks. What makes this problem even more complex is that the current value of stock prices, in turn, influences the course of the economy; thus stock market participants have to determine how their calculations will affect the economy. In practice, using the model is not so difficult as it may sound. But implicitly, stock market participants act as if they perform all these rather complicated calculations.

As a historical note, models that combine rational asset markets and nonrational goods markets were first used by Dornbusch (1976) to discuss issues concerning the behavior of foreign exchange. The phase diagram techniques that we will use in examining the properties of the model have become a basic tool in all fields of economics in which rational expectations are an important feature of the model.

The analysis begins by outlining behavior in the two basic sectors, the goods market and asset markets. These sectors are then combined to discuss the long-run equilibrium of the system and the behavior of the model with anticipated and unanticipated changes in policy.

In the goods market the private sector and the government purchase goods and services. Following the view of James Tobin, private spending by both consumers and firms depends on the value of stock market wealth. As stock prices increase, consumers find their wealth increasing and increase spending while firms find it more advantageous to engage in new investments as the stock market signals their increased value. We will focus on the short run in which the capital stock will be taken as fixed – ignoring the effect of new investment on the capital stock. Because the capital stock is fixed, we can choose units of measurement so that it identically equals one. If the price per unit of capital is q, then the value of the stock market will also be q.

Private spending, $a(q)$, is an increasing function of stock market wealth. Government spending, g, is exogenous. Thus at any point in time, total spending is $a(q) + g$. The dynamic behavior in the goods market depends on the relationship between total spending and currently produced output. If total spending equals currently produced output, the goods market is in equilibrium. If not, then output will adjust. If current spending exceeds output, then firms will find their inventory stocks falling and will step up production. If spending falls short of output, then inventories will pile up and firms will cut production. This adjustment process is precisely the same one described in elementary macroeconomic textbooks and has no particular relation to the rational expectations hypothesis.

We can summarize this behavior with the following dynamic equation

$$\dot{y} = \alpha[a(q) + g - y] \qquad (3.1)$$

The term in brackets is the excess of spending over current income. The coefficient α translates this into the rate of change of output. It will be useful to present a graphical interpretation of equation (3.1). In Figure 3.1 the $\dot{y} = 0$ locus is drawn in q-y space. When $\dot{y} = 0$, the goods market is in equilibrium and spending equals output. The locus is upward sloping because a higher value of stock market wealth q induces higher spending and a higher level of output is needed to maintain equilibrium. Above the $\dot{y} = 0$ locus spending exceeds output, inventories are decreasing, and output is increasing; below the locus spending falls short of output, inventories

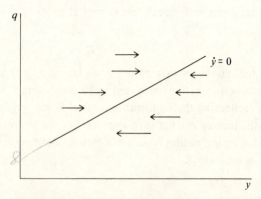

Figure 3.1   The goods market. The $\dot{y} = 0$ locus depicts the pairs of q, y where spending equals output.

are accumulating, and output is falling. The arrows in the phase diagram depict these movements in y.

The financial sector of the model is a bit more complicated. The three assets in the economy are money, short-term bonds, and equities. Money (M) bears no return and has no purchasing power risk because the price level is fixed. Short-term bonds function like savings accounts, paying an instantaneous yield of r with no revaluation of principal. The anticipated yield on equities consists of two parts: (1) Holders of equity receive profits from capital invested. (2) There is a potential for capital gains or losses on the existing shares of equity. If the price of a share is q, the anticipated yield on equities equals

$$\begin{matrix} \text{anticipated} \\ \text{yield} \end{matrix} = \frac{\pi}{q} + \frac{\dot{q}^{\epsilon}}{q} = \begin{matrix} \text{profits} \\ \text{per share} \end{matrix} + \begin{matrix} \text{anticipated} \\ \text{capital gains} \end{matrix} \qquad (3.2)$$

Except for moments during which the authorities announce new monetary or fiscal policies, investors will be assumed to forecast capital gains or losses on existing stock perfectly – this is the *perfect foresight assumption*. In a deterministic model, such as this example, it is the analogue to the rational expectations assumption. It means that, except for times at which new policies are announced, anticipated capital gains will equal actual capital gains or

$$\frac{\dot{q}}{q} = \frac{\dot{q}^e}{q} \qquad (3.3)$$

The demand for money in this model is an increasing function of income (reflecting transactions motives) and a decreasing function of interest rates (reflecting the opportunity cost of holding money). Equilibrium in the money market then implies that the interest rate can be expressed as an increasing function of income and a decreasing function of the money stock.

$$r = zy - hM \qquad (3.4)$$

Short-term bonds and equity are assumed to be perfect substitutes in investor's portfolios. Goods that are perfect substitutes must sell for the same price or, for assets, must earn the same return. This means that at every point in time arbitrage ensures that the holding yield on the two securities must be equal:

$$r = \frac{\pi}{q} + \frac{\dot{q}}{q} \qquad (3.5)$$

Profits will be described as an increasing linear function of the level of income:

$$\pi = \alpha_0 + \alpha_1 y \qquad (3.6)$$

Substituting the expressions for interest rates and profits into the arbitrage relation (3.5) yields the dynamic equation for the asset market:

$$zy - hM = \frac{\alpha_0 + \alpha_1 y}{q} + \frac{\dot{q}}{q}$$

or $\qquad (3.7)$

$$\dot{q} = q\underbrace{[zy - hM]}_{r} - \underbrace{(\alpha_0 + \alpha_1 y)}_{\pi}$$

We can again draw the appropriate phase diagram for this dynamic relation. The $\dot{q} = 0$ locus in q-y space is the locus of points along which there are no capital gains or losses. In that case the short-

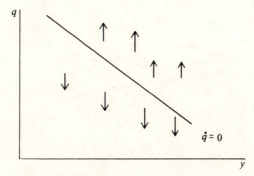

Figure 3.2   Asset market equilibrium. The $\dot{q} = 0$ locus gives pairs of q and y consistent with asset market equilibrium and no capital gains.

term interest rate r must equal profits per share:

$$(\dot{q} = 0 \text{ locus}) \qquad r = \frac{\pi}{q} \tag{3.8}$$

Because both interest rates (via the demand for money) and profits are increasing functions of income, the slope of the $\dot{q} = 0$ locus in q-y space is ambiguous. Solely for expositional purposes, we will assume that profits are not very sensitive to income (α_1 is small), which ensures the downward-sloping line in Figure 3.2. The implication of this assumption is that higher levels of income will depress the stock market. Although profits rise with income, interest rates also rise, and the depressing effect of higher interest rates is assumed to be the dominant factor.

Above the $\dot{q} = 0$ locus the interest rate on bonds exceeds profits per share. To maintain market equilibrium, share prices must be increasing to provide enough capital gains to make investors indifferent between holding equity and bonds. Below the $\dot{q} = 0$ locus profits per share exceed interest rates and investors must expect capital losses to maintain asset market equilibrium. Thus the price of equities must be falling below the locus. The economic intuition for this pattern is straightforward. At any level of income a very high level of stock prices means that earnings (or dividends) per

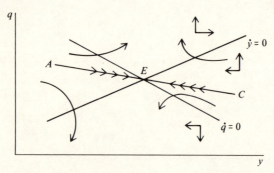

Figure 3.3 Complete phase diagram. At all points, except along the line AC, the system will diverge from the equilibrium E.

share are low. Consequently, investors must be expecting capital gains if they are to be indifferent between holding bonds and equities. Similarly, a low level of stock prices means that earnings per share are high. If earnings (or dividends) per share exceed the interest rate, all investors would rush to purchase equities unless they expect some capital losses on stocks.

Putting the two graphs together gives a complete picture of the dynamics. Figure 3.3 contains the full phase diagram with representative paths for stock prices and output. For every point in the diagram the dynamic equations of motion dictate the paths for the variables. At the intersection of the two curves both $\dot{y}$ and $\dot{q}$ are equal to zero because spending is equal to output and earnings per share equal the interest rate. This is the long-run equilibrium for the model.

The phase diagram exhibits what is termed saddle-point instability – for almost all points in the space, the trajectories lead away from the intersection of the two loci, with the exception of those points along the line AC. If q and y lie along this line, both variables converge to the long-run equilibrium.

Although in some economic contexts instability of economic processes are feared, in rational expectations models the instability of the formal system is used to determine the actual trajectories that the system will follow. We will *assume* that the system will return to long-run equilibrium following any shock. As the phase diagram indicates, if the system did not return to the long-run equilibrium, then the value of shares and output would go to either zero or infinity. These outcomes are ruled out by assumption. Although this assumption may seem arbitrary, there are two rationales for it. First, it can be viewed as a version of Samuelson's Correspondence Principle. As Paul Samuelson (1965) has argued, it does not make sense to do comparative statics on unstable models. By assuming stability, one can often obtain interesting economic insights. Second, in models in which there is explicit maximizing behavior it is often possible to prove that the utility maximizing path is, in fact, the one that converges to the unique equilibrium. Brock (1975) provides an interesting illustration of this principle in a simple monetary model. This assumption about stability should not be misinterpreted. We are not denying that economic systems cannot be unstable. We are, however, suggesting that comparative static or dynamic exercises are not really meaningful or interesting with unstable models.

For any given value of output there is only one share price that is consistent with the system returning to long-run equilibrium. That share price can be found by finding the value of q along the line AC at the prevailing level of output. In our subsequent analysis, investors will always price equities so that the price lies along line AC and the system returns to the long-run equilibrium.

The share price, in fact, is the present discounted value of future profits streams. The arbitrage or equal-yield condition, equation (3.5), is a differential equation in the share price, q. Integrating the equation forward yields the following solution:

$$q_t = \int_t^\infty \pi_s \exp \left[- \int_t^s r(v) \, dv \right] ds \tag{3.9}$$

This expression states that the share price at any point in time is the present discounted value of future profits where both profits and interest rates vary over time as the economy approaches the long-run equilibrium.

Equipped with these phase diagrams, we are prepared to analyze the effects of changes in the money stock. We can distinguish between

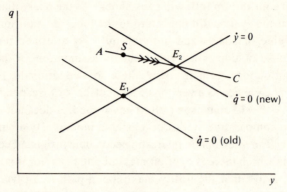

Figure 3.4   An unanticipated increase in the money stock. Stock prices jump to point S and then decrease as output and stock prices move to the new equilibrium E_2.

two types of changes in the money stock: unanticipated and anticipated changes.

Consider first an unanticipated change in the money stock when the system is originally in the long-run equilibrium E_1 as depicted in Figure 3.4. When the money stock is increased, the $\dot{q} = 0$ locus shifts up, reflecting the fact that, at any level of income, interest rates will be lower, and hence share prices will be higher along the new $\dot{q} = 0$ locus.

The new long-run equilibrium position is E_2 and has a higher level of income and stock prices than the original equilibrium E_1. Because prices are fixed, an increase in the nominal money stock increases the real money supply and therefore interest rates fall. Lower interest rates stimulate wealth, leading to higher spending and higher output. As output increases, profits increase, further enhancing wealth. These long-run results are quite conventional and would be expected in any fixed-price Keynesian model.

The transition to the new equilibrium is more interesting. When the money stock is increased, the $\dot{q} = 0$ locus shifts and the new stable line AC now lies above the old equilibrium E_1. Because output adjusts only slowly, stock prices must jump immediately to point S. Stock prices then fall and output increases until the new long-run equilibrium E_2 is reached. Stock prices, therefore, *overshoot* the new long-run equilibrium, rising temporarily above their long-run value. What is the economic intuition behind this result?

When the money stock is increased, the interest rate immediately falls to equilibrate the money market. Everyone in the economy recognizes that, as income increases, the increased demand for money will raise interest rates during the transition to long-run equilibrium. Equity yields must also be increasing during this transition period to maintain equilibrium in the asset market. The way equity yields are primarily increased is through a fall in share prices, thereby increasing profits per share. However, the new long-run equilibrium share price lies above the old equilibrium. Therefore, share prices must jump immediately *above* the long-run equilibrium and decline during the transition. This ensures that (1) in the long run the new share price lies above the share price at the old equilibrium and (2) during the approach to the new equilibrium equity yields are increasing to maintain equality with rising interest rates.

This result can be viewed from another perspective. In the new long-run equilibrium share prices are higher primarily because of lower interest rates. Short-term interest rates are, in fact, at their lowest level immediately after the increase in the money stock. As output begins to increase, short-term interest rates are bid up, reflecting the increased transactions demand for money. This means that stock prices will be at their highest level immediately after the increase in the money stock and then fall as profits are discounted by successively higher interest rates. Therefore stock prices immediately jump above their long-run equilibrium value and fall on the path toward the new equilibrium.

This "overshooting" phenomenon is a property of other models that combine efficient financial markets and nonrational goods markets. Indeed, Dornbusch's (1976) original paper on this topic was motivated by what appeared to be excessive fluctuations in foreign exchange markets. Dornbusch argued that the short-run overshooting of long-run equilibrium that emerged from his model was a possible explanation for the observed volatility of exchange rates.

The dynamics of an anticipated change in the money stock are even more intriguing. Although the long-run equilibrium position remains the same as in the unanticipated case, the transition to the

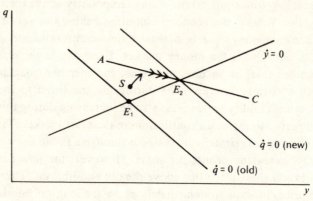

Figure 3.5 An anticipated increase in the money stock. At $t = 0$ stock prices jump to S so that prices and income will reach the AC line at $t = T$.

new equilibrium is quite different. To fix ideas, suppose that at time $t = t_0$ it is announced that the money stock will be increased at a later time $t = T$.

Figure 3.5 contains the appropriate phase diagrams to analyze this case. There are three basic points to keep in mind to understand this case. First, the $\dot{q} = 0$ locus shifts only when the money stock is actually increased at time T because it is a function of the prevailing money stock. Second, it is inconsistent with profit-maximizing arbitrage for the price of equities to jump at that time. If the price of equities jumped, it would be possible to make infinite capital gains by investing just a little money an instant before the increase. This is recognized by speculators who bid up prices so that no jumps occur. Finally, after time T, the system must be on the stable line AC if it is to return to the new equilibrium.

When the money supply increase is announced, stock prices jump to point S. This point is chosen so that as the share prices and income follow their dynamic trajectories, the share price will be on the line AC at time T when the money supply is actually increased. Jumps in the price are allowed when an announcement is made because that represents new information, but they are not allowed when an announced policy is actually implemented. As the graph indicates, share prices and income both increase *before* the money supply is increased; after the money supply is increased, output continues to increase but share prices fall.

The economics of the situation are fascinating. When the money supply increase is announced, economic actors know that this will mean higher income and profits, along with lower interest rates in the long run. As this is discounted back to the present, stock prices will rise, reflecting the higher present value of the profit stream. Higher stock prices, in turn, stimulate spending, which leads to an increase in output *before* the money stock is actually increased. To an outside observer who is not privy to the money supply announcement, this looks like a case of rampant stock market speculation fueling a boom in the economy. Since interest rates rise during the first phase, it may appear that the Fed is forced to increase the money stock to accommodate the increased money demand. This example illustrates the pitfalls awaiting an unsophisticated researcher who is searching for the lag between changes in money and changes in output. In the case of an anticipated increase in the money supply, there is, in fact, a *lead* relationship – changes in output precede changes in the money stock.

With this case it is possible to illustrate the rather troubling phenomenon of multiple rational expectation equilibrium. Imagine that at time $t = 0$ the Fed announces the following policy: "If interest rates rise between time 0 and time T, the money supply will be increased at time T; if not, the money stock will remain constant." A moment of reflection shows that this is consistent with two different equilibrium paths. It is certainly consistent with the previous example because interest rates would rise in anticipation of the increase in the money stock that, according to this policy, will actually transpire. On the other hand, another consistent outcome is for interest rates to remain constant, in which case the money stock will not be increased at time T and the system will remain forever at the old equilibrium.

The issues surrounding multiple expectational equilibrium are rather technical and cannot be dealt with here. In this example

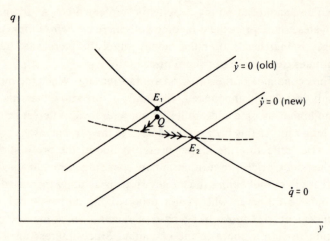

Figure 3.6   Anticipated increase in government spending. When the increase in government spending is announced, stock prices fall and output falls until the time when government expenditure actually increases.

the multiple equilibrium arose because of the specification of policy. Sargent and Wallace (1975) find that the price level is indeterminate in a classical model when the Fed pegs the interest rate. Multiple equilibria can also occur when the equations of the model have certain other properties. Taylor (1977) and Shiller (1978) provide detailed discussions of these issues.

Returning to the basic model, it is also possible to analyze increases in government spending. Figure 3.6 contains the appropriate phase diagram for an *anticipated* increase in government expenditure. First note that the $\dot{y} = 0$ locus shifts down when the increase in government spending actually transpires. In the new long-run equilibrium, output is higher but stock prices are lower. The reason that stock prices are lower is that the increase in government spending raises output and causes an increase in the demand for money. The increase in the demand for money causes interest rates to rise to equilibrate the money market. Higher interest rates offset the effect of higher profits and lead to a lower level of equilibrium stock prices.

The dynamics of the situation reflect the fact that stock prices will be lower in the future. As the increase in government spending is announced, market participants anticipate higher interest rates and stock prices immediately fall to Q. But with lower stock prices, spending is reduced and output actually begins to fall. The fall in output actually continues until the time that government spending is increased, at which time output increases to the new equilibrium. The implications for stabilization policy are rather striking: Announced fiscal expansions can initially have contractionary effects.

We have seen that for a model in which only the asset markets are rational, the distinction between anticipated and unanticipated still matters. Although the long-run equilibrium of the system will not differ from traditional models, the approach to equilibrium and the dynamics of the economic system are dramatically affected by an announcement of a policy. Moreover, in this model the stock market participants implicitly need to understand the complete structure of the model to determine the proper course for stock prices. If stock market participants must figure out the structure of the model, so must the economist who is trying to understand their behavior.

Traditional macro models neither distinguish between anticipated and unanticipated policy changes nor have even one group of actors calculating the future course of the economy in a rational manner by using the full model. In the two respects these macro models are deficient in describing a world in which just some economic actors are rational. Models in which only some sectors of the economy exhibit rational behavior differ in their implications from those models in which all sectors are rational. However, the techniques of analysis are markedly similar for both types of models.

It would be valuable to know what empirical difference it makes with our current econometric models if the financial sectors are assumed to be rational. For example, Does an anticipated increase in the money supply operate faster when the financial markets are constrained to be consistent with rational behavior? Fortunately, we have some evidence on this issue.

To explore this question, Ray Fair (1979) used an econometric model that he had previously developed. In Fair's model there were both an equation explaining stock prices and an equation explaining long-term bond yields in terms of short-term yields (a term-structure equation). Fair reworked his model so that these two equations were consistent with rational behavior. Both his methods and results deserve attention.

Fair's term-structure equation is based on what is known as the "expectations theory." According to this theory, the return from holding an n-period security is equal to the expected return from holding a series of one-period securities over the n-period horizon. This theory is based on the belief that investors are only interested in the expected returns from holding bonds and have no particular preference for holding any maturity per se. Letting R_t denote the yield to maturity on the long-run bond, we see that the theory states

$$(1 + R_t)^n = (1 + {}_tr_t^\epsilon)(1 + {}_tr_{t+1}^\epsilon) \cdots (1 + {}_tr_{t+n}^\epsilon) \qquad (3.10)$$

where ${}_tr_{t+k}^\epsilon$ are the one-period interest rates expected, at time t, to prevail in period $t + k$.

To implement this model empirically, one must specify how the expectations of the one-period interest rates are formed. In conventional macro models these expectations are based on some function of past interest rates and, perhaps, other variables. The problem with this approach is that for any given policy simulation, there is no reason to believe that the actual future interest rates will even come close to the expected rates. The rational expectations approach used by Fair goes to the opposite extreme: The actual future interest rates are constrained to equal the expected rates. Through an iterative technique, Fair ensured that in his policy simulations the actual future course of interest rates was consistent with what was anticipated.

There is another way to explain his approach. If future interest rates differed from what was expected, there would be capital gains or losses on long-term bonds. Thus Fair's method for analyzing the effects of policy was based on the principle that, in rational financial market, participants will price assets so that there will be no expected capital gains or losses. Of course, unexpected events such as the announcement of a new policy or a disturbance to the economy could cause unexpected capital revaluations, but once this unexpected event has transpired, there should be no further reasons for unanticipated capital gains on long-term bonds.

The same principle also applies to the stock market. In Fair's model stock prices are equal to the present discounted value of future after-tax profits. In his policy simulations Fair ensures that the price of stocks is consistent with the future course of profits and interest rates so that there are no capital gains or losses on equities. Again, unexpected events can cause capital gains, but once the event has occurred, financial market participants work through the consequences for interest rates and profits and calculate the appropriate level of stock prices.

Fair performed several experiments with his model. He analyzed the effects of unanticipated changes in government spending and the money supply with and without the assumption that expectations in the financial markets are formed rationally. His basic result is that the effect of these policies on the level of real output is approximately cut in half when expectations are formed rationally. The reason for this result is straightforward. There is built into the structure of his model an equation that describes the behavior of the Fed, in which the Fed's policy is to dampen economic fluctuations, or ''lean against the wind.'' When government spending is increased, the participants in the model know that the Fed is going to counteract some of the increase in output that is induced by the change in government spending. Interest rates on long-term bonds immediately rise to reflect this, and the increase in interest rates dampens spending and hence, the increase in output. It is the private sector's knowledge that the Fed *will* dampen economic fluctuations that, in fact, actually does dampen the response of the economy to exogenous shocks. If the Fed's rule had been procyclical, as some observers claim, the effects of unanticipated changes in fiscal and monetary policy would be exacerbated. In that case market participants would immediately react to the anticipated monetary policy, and the effects of shocks would be increased.

Fair's analysis of the case of an anticipated increase in government spending is interesting. His simulation technique was to announce in the year 1958 that there would be an increase in government spending taking place in 1971. Before 1971 output actually decreased and then mildly increased after 1971, for a total net effect of only one-fourth of the expansion that would have been generated if expectations were not rational. The reason for these effects is again straightforward. Economic actors know that the increase in government spending will raise short-term interest rates in the future. Because future short-term interest rates are expected to increase, current long-term interest rates rise to reflect this, and in the process, spending is decreased and output falls. When government spending increases, output increases, but the net effect is much smaller than the nonrational case.

There is another way to explain this curious result from an anticipated fiscal policy action. It is well known that, even in conventional Keynesian models, increases in government spending reduce or *crowd-out* private spending through the effect of government spending on interest rates. In traditional Keynesian models this crowding-out effect occurs at the same time as government spending changes. When a fiscal policy is announced in advance and financial market participants are rational, interest rates rise in anticipation of higher government spending and the crowding-out of private spending occurs before the level of government spending is actually increased.

Fair's analysis suggests that the quantitative effect of recognizing rational financial markets may be quite important. The precise effects, of course, would vary with the econometric model used and the stage in the business cycle when the events occur. For unanticipated events or shocks to the system the magnitude of the effects on output in the rational case as opposed to the nonrational case depends intimately on the nature of the policy rules of the authorities. As we noted, a policy of leaning against the wind was quite effective in the rational expectations case because long-term interest rates and stock prices responded immediately to the anticipated effects of these policies. However, knowledge that authorities will adopt destabilizing policies would increase the sensitivity of the economy to shocks.

Perverse effects of policy announcements are possible. As we have seen, an announced increase in government spending can actually lead to a fall in private spending and output as interest rates rise and stock prices fall in response to expected future increases in short-term interest rates. A similar theoretical result arose in Blanchard's model. From the theoretical model and Fair's empirical results we are led to a strong conclusion: Existing macro models that fail to incorporate rational financial markets can seriously mislead economists in forecasting developments *if* financial markets, to the first approximation, are rational.

Although these results are interesting and important, they fail to address the question of whether models that mix rational and non-rational elements are the proper focus of future research. Labor and product markets are generally not "auction" markets but clearly are also not totally governed by chance and caprice. Should efforts be made to model their behavior in a manner that is consistent with rational expectations? As evidenced by the discussion of alternative aggregate supply models in Chapter 2, this issue is far from resolved. Another problem with the type of mixture considered here is that stock prices probably do not simply reflect discounted expected future earnings or dividends, as our discussion in the next chapter will reveal. We are left, unfortunately, not with a solution but with a warning about the use of existing econometric models.

Rules, authorities, and the consistency of optimal policy

The techniques of optimal control, developed extensively in the 1960s, were applied to a wide range of economic models, including those in which expectations figured prominently. Yet no articles appeared in the optimal control literature suggesting that expectations created any particular type of problem or even raised any special considerations. The reason for this lack of concern about expectations and optimal control theory can be explained by the techniques employed to model expectation formation.

Perhaps the simplest possible vehicle to illustrate this point is the following equation model:

$$y_t = a_{1\ t-1}y_t^\epsilon + g_t + \epsilon_t \qquad a_1 < 1 \qquad (3.11)$$

in which an endogenous variable (y_t) is explained by individuals' expectation of the endogenous variable $(_{t-1}y_t^\epsilon)$, a government policy variable (g_t), and a random disturbance (ϵ_t). Traditional optimal control theory determines the choice for the policy variable to maximize a function that describes the preferences of policymakers. The public's expectation of the endogenous variable is assumed to be given to the policymakers, independent of their decisions.

Expectations are taken as given by policymakers for these exercises because they are assumed to be based only on the past history of the economy. This, of course, does not preclude that expectations are a complicated function of many variables, but it does imply that, at any moment of time, expectations can be described as *predetermined variables*. A wide variety of expectation formation mechanisms can be used with this approach. The adaptive expectations hypothesis, for example, implies that expectations can be expressed as a weighted average of all past values for a variable and, thus, as functions of the past history of the economy.

Treating expectations as predetermined variables has several advantages. First, expectations can be treated in the same way as any other predetermined variables – there is no need for any special procedures. Second, expectations can be modeled with a wide variety of methods as long as they can be described as some function of the past history of the economy. Finally, the current values for expectations are given independent of the choice for the policy variables.

Treating expectations as predetermined, however, negates the whole thrust of rational expectations. Expectations of endogenous variables should be responsive to current and future choices for policy variables. To assume otherwise is to limit the potential information that is available to economic actors arbitrarily and to remove from economic analysis a whole range of interesting ideas and problem.

Rather than treating expectations as predetermined variables, they can be related to the expected values of future policy variables. As an example, the simple "model" of equation (3.11) can be used to calculate the rationally expected values for the endogenous variable. Taking conditional expectations of both sides of the equation and rearranging gives the following expression.

$$_{t-1}y_t^\epsilon = \frac{1}{1-a_1}[_{t-1}g_t^\epsilon] \tag{3.12}$$

The rationally expected value for the endogenous variable ($_{t-1}y_t^\epsilon$) is thus a function of the expected value of the control variable ($_{t-1}g_t^\epsilon$), given the information available at time $t-1$. Expectations are not independent of the choices of the policy variables but are related to anticipated values for the policy variables. Policymakers must take into account the impact of their proposed actions on the public's expectations.

Policymakers can still calculate "optimal" policies when expectations are formed rationally but the procedures differ from those in which expectations are treated as predetermined. First, policymakers must propose a set of policy rules that they will follow in the future. These rules may be complicated and allow the authorities to offset shocks, but the rules must be known to the public. Given these policy rules, the private sector is then assumed to choose its course of action in line with its own objectives. Policymakers can then explore the consequences of alternative *rules* on the behavior of the private sector and can choose the rule that yields the preferred outcome. Instead of selecting policy variables taking expectations as given, expectations themselves must be modeled as functions of the proposed policy rules.

It was discovered that, by using this revised procedure to determine optimal policy, optimal plans could be *inconsistent*. To understand what this means, consider planning a course of action, at time 0, for times $t = 0, \ldots, S$, taking into account all the possible contingencies that might arise over the planning period. In period 1, again calculate optimal plans for $t = 1, \ldots, S$, also accounting for possible contingencies. There are now two different plans for periods 1 through S, one formulated at time 0 and another formulated at time 1. If these plans differ in any way, the optimal policy for this problem is termed inconsistent.

Perhaps the best way to understand the problem of inconsistency is to begin with what seems to be a truism: "Whatever situation policymakers inherit, they should use their policy tools to pick the best course of action." This appears to be a rather innocuous statement.

In certain situations, however, this truism gives rather peculiar advice. Consider the case of patent policy. In order to encourage research and spur inventions, the government offers patent protection or, equivalently, the monopoly of a new product for a limited period of time. After the product has been invented, policy considerations change. The truism suggests that the best policy would be to abolish all monopoly rights to the manufacture and sale of the new product. After all, we have inherited a situation in which the product has already been invented. It is in the interest of society to have the product sold in a competitive market rather than by a monopolist who will restrict supply. The logic of the truism seems to dictate that there should be no patent protection.

There are other similar examples. Take the case of an "excess-profits" tax on holders of grain inventories whenever a shortage exists. The fear of an excess-profits tax on profits from grain storage may impede storage activities, but once grain has been brought to storage, no disincentive effects arise from a tax on profits. Indeed, because there are no perverse incentive effects, it makes sense for the government to raise revenue this way. *Given that the grain has been stored*, taxing excess profits is a good policy.

Something seems wrong in both examples. If people knew that patent protection was going to be systematically stripped away, inventive activities would drop sharply. If profits from grain speculation were always taxed away, no one would undertake storage activities. It seems appropriate for the government to insist that patents will be respected and "excess profits" will not be subject to tax. In this way the government can induce private behavior that is desirable. But once the government has induced this behavior, it has the temptation to cheat, reneging on patent protection and taxing profits. Optimal policies in these cases are *inconsistent*. Viewed at time 0, the best policy for the future is to protect patents and avoid taxing excess profits. After inventions have been discovered and grain stored, the best policy is to refuse to honor patents and to tax profits.

An extended example from the field of taxation, based on work by Fischer (1980), can shed further light on these issues. Consider a simple two-period world in which individuals inherit a capital stock in the first period, work in both periods, and save in the first period. The only vehicle of saving is capital so that the capital stock in period 2 equals the total savings from the first period. The government provides a public good to all individuals and must raise tax revenue for this purpose. The key question to be answered is what type of taxes will be levied in each period to finance the public good.

A rational expectations equilibrium in this model is a competitive equilibrium in which the private sector knows and responds to the taxes that will be imposed in both periods. The government is free to announce different tax rates, observe private sector behavior, and then announce the tax policy that gives the highest utility to a representative individual. In general, the optimal tax policy will be to announce that *both* labor and capital will be taxed in the second period. If taxes fall solely on capital, individuals would save very little in the first period, and instead, would increase their consumption. If returns from capital are heavily taxed in period 2, there is little incentive for saving. If individuals save little, then the second period capital stock will be low and total societal output will also be low. Taxes, however, should not be placed exclusively on labor because, as long as labor supply is responsive to wages, the labor–leisure choice will be distorted. For this reason, optimal policies will generally involve taxing both capital and labor to ensure that individuals save enough.

In the second period, however, the government will be tempted to change its mind and tax just capital. Capital is supplied inelastically in the second period, but laborers will, in general, have some elasticity in their labor supply. Since David Ricardo, economists have recognized that, ideally, taxes should fall on factors that are supplied inelastically. The reason for this is simple: If a factor is supplied inelastically, a tax will not change the quantity supplied and thus there are no economic distortions created by the imposition of a tax. On the other hand, taxing an elastically supplied factor, such as labor in this example, will cause distortions. Viewed from the vantage point of the second period, the government's best policy is to tax capital, a policy that will raise revenue but cause no distortions. Hence the optimal policy in this simple example is inconsistent.

The only consistent policy in this case is to tax only capital in the second period. That policy, however, will generally not be optimal because private savings, and hence the second period capital stock, will be too low. The welfare of the representative individual will be lower under this consistent policy than in a rational expectations equilibrium in which both labor and capital income are subject to tax.

If people believe the government will tax both capital and labor in period 2, the government can make the representative individual better off by taxing only capital in the second period. Of course, a *repeated* policy of breaking promises would destroy the belief of the private sector in the government, private savings would dry up, and welfare would be sharply reduced. It is interesting that a repeated history of broken promises would lead to the consistent, but suboptimal, plan. One possibility is that it might be advantageous for the government to break its promise only on occasion – a possibility we will return to later.

Several points about this example deserve emphasis. First, inconsistency of optimal plans can arise even when the objective function of the government is identical to that of the representative individual. Second, inconsistency can also occur if expectations are not fully rational. As long as expectations are just somewhat responsive to proposed policy variables, inconsistency can occur. Finally, it is possible to calculate the optimal policy as long as the endogeneity of expectations is accounted for in the optimization problem.

Not all models in which agents have rational expectations will have optimal policies that are inconsistent. The general message that seems to emerge from the literature is that as long as there are no nondistorting taxes, then optimal policies will be inconsistent. If there is a possibility of using lump-sum or other forms of non-distorting taxation, optimal policies will be consistent. Although the examples that have been presented have been primarily from tax policy, Calvo (1978) has shown that similar results hold in models of monetary economies.

Early work on this topic by Kydland and Prescott (1977) and Prescott (1977) advertised it as the death of optimal control theory. This was somewhat misleading. It is true that traditional control theory, which treated expectations as predetermined, was inadequate to deal with models in which expectations were formed rationally. Control theory has to be done differently in this case, but it is still possible to choose among different policies.

How is this related to the question of rules versus discretion? In the literature, discretion has been associated with the truism of choosing the best policy, *given* that you have inherited a particular situation. In our last example the discretionary policy in the second period was to place all the burden of taxation on capital. Rules, on the other hand, are associated with maintaining the rational expectations equilibrium – that is, honoring patents, not taxing "excess profits" and taxing both labor and capital in the second period. Because optimal policies are often inconsistent, it is important that rules be honored. If rules are systematically broken, then, as we have seen, the private sector response may not be desirable.

There are really two different issues here. First, some type of rules for policy are necessary simply to be able to predict the response of the private sector. Predictable private sector behavior is predicated on at least some type of stable framework for policy decisions. Second, even in this framework optimal policies will be inconsistent; that is, there will always be temptations to break the rules seemingly to improve private welfare.

The argument supporting the superiority of rules goes back to Henry Simons's 1936 article, "Rules Versus Authorities in Monetary

Policy.'' For Simons, the issues were clearly political and of the highest order of importance:

> For the present, we obviously must rely on a large measure of discretionary money management . . . Such a policy, however, must be guided by a more fundamental strategy . . . otherwise, political control must degenerate into endless concessions to organized minorities, with gradual undermining of the ''constitutional structure'' under which free enterprise and representative government can function. (1936:15)

Because it will always seem advantageous in the short run to break rules, democracy might degenerate. The concern of some of today's economists is expressed less dramatically in the language of modern science: Breaking rules may lead to consistent, but suboptimal, policies.

The basic counterargument in this debate is that ''discretion'' has been narrowly caricatured. Discretionary policies have been associated with actions that myopically break long-honored rules and commitments. Advocates of discretion could argue that discretionary policies work best in a stable framework of rules. For example, in actual patent policy, there are many discretionary decisions that have to be made in applying the general rules of policies. Indeed, it is hard to conceive of rules that could exist without discretionary interpretation. Congress can certainly not write simple rules for tax policy – otherwise the Internal Revenue Service would not have to issue volume of regulations. Even less imperfect sources than Congress face this problem – the Ten Commandments had to be supplemented by the volumes of the Talmud.

The traditional argument against relying solely on rules is simply that it is impossible to write rules that can cover all possible contingencies. Part of this problem arises because there are many complex contingencies that can arise. More fundamentally, conceptual frameworks change and perceptions of contingencies change accordingly. One prominent example of this is the OPEC price increases. Before the dramatic 1973 price increases, ''supply shocks'' were virtually absent from the macroeconomic dialogue. It would have been impossible ex ante to write rules for monetary policy when supply shocks hit because these shocks were simply not in the realm of policy discourse.

Despite these well-known and traditional arguments against strict reliance on rules, the inconsistency issue does strengthen the basic case for using rules in conducting tax and macroeconomic policy. In practical terms, this means attempting to formulate a policy to deal with all recessions or booms and not simply concocting a policy for a particular incident. This is easier said than done. There is a natural inclination among policymakers to view the *differences* between situations rather than the common features. For example, the 1974–5 recession was viewed partly as stemming from rapid inventory decumulation, whereas the recession of 1980 was attributed to tight money and credit policies with little role for autonomous inventory movements. For a policy of rules to gain acceptance, policymakers must be willing to focus on the common features of business fluctuations rather than on the idiosyncracies. Policy planning would have to be reoriented with more concentration on longer run issues and less preoccupation with current affairs. Seasoned political observers would be quite skeptical of any such transformation.

Earlier we raised the possibility of a policy that adheres to rules but allows for the possibility of certain extreme events in which the rules can be temporarily suspended. For example, the government may pledge that it will not nationalize or commandeer industrial facilities in normal times. This should alleviate industry fears and promote capital accumulation. However, in a state of national emergency, it may be in everyone's interest to allow the government to take control of key facilities. To prevent national "emergencies" from becoming an everyday occurrence, one would find it useful to place institutional impediments so that frivolous emergencies can be avoided. One possibility would be to write an explicit rule in which the Congress had to declare a war before any industrial facilities were seized. As long as there were sufficient costs to the act of declaring a war, society could be assured a healthy climate for capital accumulation along with protection in true emergencies.

In this example, rather than allowing for violations of the rule, the rule has been rewritten. It may not be possible in all cases to write these general rules. However, the basic point still remains – as long as the government faces some constraints in breaking promises, the opportunity for the government to break rules can be very valuable.

The often maligned process of formulating tax policy approaches this ideal in its better moments. Changes in the tax law are made infrequently and there are sufficient obstacles (interest groups, congressional hearings) to prevent capricious changes. When changes in tax laws are made, they have to filter through the long, legislative process. In the legislative dialogue ''fairness'' is an important criterion used to evaluate changes and can be linked to honoring promises and not to reneging on commitments. The imperatives of fair treatment reduce the possibilities for inconsistent tax changes.

Until recently monetary policy seemed to be conducted with complete discretion, with policy tools adjusted to the latest perceptions of credit conditions. Congress, however, has begun to pressure the Fed to adopt targets and goals for money growth. Currently the Fed must report regularly to Congress and discuss the reasons for not meeting its stated goals. This adds a rulelike element to the Fed's behavior but still preserves the ability of the Fed to act decisively in times of financial panics or extreme business conditions. Disagreements, of course, will still arise over how ''extreme'' business conditions really are. Again, this is part of the basic dilemma: We want to tie the hand of authorities in normal times to ensure a stable policy environment, but we want our authorities to be able to act decisively in crises. These demands are also inconsistent, albeit in a different sense.

Econometric policy evaluation

Another strong argument for the use of rules by policy authorities comes from a different source. In a penetrating article Robert E. Lucas (1976) analyzed the uses and abuses of existing econometric work for policy evaluation and arrived at a rather startling conclusion. ''The only *scientific* quantitative evaluations available to us are comparisons of the consequences of alternative policy rules . . . simulations [of existing models] can, in principle provide *no* useful information as to the actual consequences of alternative economic policies'' (1976:41, 20). Without a reliance on rules and models that can handle them, it is virtually impossible to do any sophisticated policy analysis.

Lucas arrived at this rather dramatic conclusion by examining the nature of the equations used in typical econometric models. Current practice, he argued, is to estimate an econometric relationship (e.g., a consumption function) and then use this relationship to predict consumption behavior under alternative scenarios or patterns for income. An implicit assumption in this type of exercise is that the econometric relationship will remain stable under the different scenarios. Lucas argued that everything we know about dynamic economic theory suggests that this assumption is false – that is, we would expect the behavioral equations in the model to change as the scenarios changed.

Changes in the behavioral relations in the equations of an econometric model arise because agents change their forecasting schemes to adapt to a new economic environment. If the environment can be characterized in some systematic manner, econometricians can hopefully use economic theory to predict how economic agents will behave. However, if the agents find the economic environment to be random and chaotic, econometricians will not be able to say much about agents' behavior. Stable policy rules that lead to a stable economic environment can give the econometrician at least a fighting chance to predict economic behavior.

Although this link to the rules versus discretion debate is intriguing, the practical message from Lucas's message is that existing econometric models are almost useless for traditional policy analysis. Traditional policy analysis assumes the economic structure will not change when different policy scenarios are imposed – Lucas suggests that this key assumption is simply erroneous.

These arguments are quite abstract, and presenting some simple examples to illustrate these points will be helpful. Fortunately, examples are easy to find because virtually every sector of a modern econometric model involves expectations. Whenever expectations are involved in an equation, we expect that agents will form them in a manner consistent with their environment. As their environment changes, so, too, their expectation formation procedures must change. Expectations enter into consumption, investment, wage–price, and financial sectors of most macro models; hence Lucas's arguments apply to virtually all sectors in macro models.

Before presenting an example of Lucas's (1976) argument, we should summarize existing econometric policy practice. Let y_{t+1} be the state of the economy in time $t + 1$ – that is, a description of all relevant characteristics of the economy. A typical econometric model can be written as

$$y_{t+1} = F(y_t, X_t, \theta, \epsilon_t) \tag{3.13}$$

The state of the economy at time $t + 1$ will be a function of the state at time t, y_t; the values of policy and other exogenous variables (X_t); shocks to the system (ϵ_t); and parameters (θ) that characterize the precise relationship.

An econometrician finds data on Y and X and then estimates the parameters θ by using various statistical techniques. Once estimates of θ are found, the model can be used for policy experiments. Policy experiments simply involve using equation (3.14) to find out the values for states of the economy (the y's) when different policy configurations (the X's) are tried. The key assumption, which Lucas challenges, is that the parameters θ will remain unchanged as the X's are systematically varied.

To illustrate Lucas's insight, we will explore a simple version of Milton Friedman's permanent income hypothesis. According to Friedman's theory, consumption decisions are based on long-run expected income and not simply on the current receipts individuals may possess at the moment. In Friedman's terms, consumption is not based on current income but on permanent income. This can be expressed as

$$C_t = k Y_t^p \tag{3.14}$$

where

$$C_t = \text{consumption}$$
$$Y_t^p = \text{permanent income}$$
$$k = \text{a constant}$$

It remains, of course, to specify how permanent income is determined. Assume that at time $t - 1$ individuals calculate the present discounted value of their expected future income stream from time t to infinity and use this as a measure of permanent income. That is,

$$Y_t^p = \sum_{s=t}^{\infty} \beta^{s-t} {}_{t-1}y_s^{\epsilon} \tag{3.15}$$

where

$$
\begin{aligned}
{}_{t-1}y_s^{\epsilon} &= \text{expected income for period } s \text{ as viewed from} \\
&\quad t - 1 \\
\beta &= \text{discount factor}
\end{aligned}
$$

Expectations of future income are made at time $t - 1$; we are implicitly assuming that consumption decisions for period t are made before actual income is known for that period. This particular formulation of the permanent income hypothesis has some technical problems [see Hall (1978)] but remains a useful vehicle to illustrate Lucas's message.

Of course, just stating that permanent income is based on the discounted value of expected future income streams does not yield a theory with any testable implications, *unless* the expectation mechanism is specified. Here we invoke the rational expectations assumption: Agents' psychological, subjective expectations equal the true mathematical expectation of future income. That is, agents are assumed to know the stochastic process governing the behavior of income and to predict their income by using this process.

The implications of this assumption can be illustrated with a few examples. Suppose that income follows a random walk or, stated differently, that changes in income from period to period are random. We can write this as

$$y_t = y_{t-1} + \omega_t \tag{3.16}$$

where ω_t = a random disturbance.

Random walks have one nice statistical property. The best estimate of income any date in the future as viewed from time $t - 1$ is simply the level of income at $t - 1$. In our notation, $y_s^e = y_{t-1}$ for all s. Although we know that future incomes most certainly will not equal y_{t-1}, their best *guess* at time $t - 1$ is still y_{t-1}.

Using this fact and the formula for permanent income [equation (3.15)], we find that permanent income is

$$\frac{1}{1 - \beta} \, y_{t-1} \tag{3.17}$$

Plugging this into the basic consumption relationship yields the consumption relation

$$C_t = \frac{k}{1 - \beta} \, y_{t-1} \tag{3.18}$$

To the untutored eye equation (3.18) does not look like a permanent income relationship at all; rather, it appears that consumption is just a simple function of last period's income. Of course, equation (3.18) states that consumption is a function of last period's income, but this occurs because that period's income is the best predictor for the whole future stream of income on which consumption decisions are based.

Now suppose that, in fact, income followed a random walk and that the permanent income hypothesis was true. Econometricians could readily estimate the consumption function and would find the relationship given by equation (3.18). Consumption would be a function of just last period's income and would be easy to predict for policy purposes.

All is fine until policymakers decide to try a new stabilization technique, which alters the process governing income. If the stochastic process governing income changes, and if econometricians try to predict consumption using equation (3.18), they will make serious mistakes.

To take an example, suppose the process governing income was changed to

$$y_t = \bar{y} + \epsilon_t \tag{3.19}$$

Equation (3.19) states that income in time t is simply a constant number ($\bar{y}$), plus random noise (ϵ_t). Assume that from the vantage point of time $t - 1$, the best prediction of ϵ_t is always zero. Then the best prediction for income in *all* future periods is simply the constant level $\bar{y}$; that is, $y_s^e = \bar{y}$ for all s.

Plugging these expectations into the permanent income equations yields a value for permanent income $Y_t^p = \bar{y}/(1 - \beta)$. Using the consumption relation again, we find that consumption each period is just a constant, or

$$C_t = \frac{k}{1 - \beta} \, \bar{y} \qquad (3.20)$$

Instead of predicting consumption by last period's income, econometricians should be using equation (3.20), which states that consumption will be constant for every period and will not be related to the actual value of the previous period's income.

These results can be summarized by writing a general consumption function:

$$C_t = \text{constant} + \alpha \, y_{t-1} \qquad (3.21)$$

In the first economy the constant was zero and $\alpha = k/1 - \beta$; in the second economy $\alpha = 0$ and the constant equaled $[k/1 - \beta]\,(\bar{y})$. As the process governing income changes, the coefficients of a typical consumption relation like equation (3.21) will also change. Lucas's criticism of econometric models is that they fail to incorporate this point – they assume that coefficients will be constant when the time-series pattern of income changes. As evident from this simple example, large errors in forecasting can occur if these issues are ignored.

Besides being an interesting illustration of Lucas's theme, the consumption function example has some historical interest. Muth, of course, developed the rational expectation theory precisely to make the point that expectations had to be endogenous and to change as the stochastic process governing variables changed. In an earlier paper entitled, ''Optimal Properties of Exponentially Weighted Forecasts,'' Muth (1960) showed that the adaptive expectation mechanism, used by Milton Friedman to implement the permanent income hypothesis empirically, would also be a procedure adopted by rational agents if the time-series process for income followed a specific stochastic process. The paper was widely cited as a justification for using an adaptive expectation formula for calculating permanent income. Today it is evident that this interpretation misrepresented Muth's analysis. If the stochastic process governing income changed to some other form, the adaptive expectation mechanisms would no longer be consistent with rational behavior.

Other examples of models in which coefficients should change abound in macroeconomics. In the discussion of Phillips curves in the last chapter it was noted that the slope of the short-run Phillips curve depended on the previous variability of the general price level. When the general price level was very variable, agents would view changes in their prices as changes in the general price level and their output response would be muted. Conversely, in an environment with a stable general price level, most changes in prices would be perceived to be changes in relative prices and agents' responses would be greater. In this case the slope of the short-run Phillips curve depends explicitly on the inflation environment.

Long-term interest rates play an important role in most macro models. They are usually linked to shorter term rates by the expectations hypothesis discussed earlier. According to this theory, long-term rates are functions of expected future short-term rates, with all rates adjusting so that anticipated holding yields from securities are the same for all maturities.

In most econometric models long-term rates are determined by a weighted average of past short-term rates with the weights determined empirically by usual regression methods. It should be evident, however, that the appropriate weights given to past interest rates depend explicitly on the stochastic processes governing short-term interest rates. To take a simple example, assume that short-term interest rates follow a random walk. If they do follow this stochastic process, then the best prediction of future short-term interest rates will simply be today's short-term rate. In other words, the best predictor of the long-term rate should be some function of just the current short-term rate and no others. On the other hand, if the stochastic process governing short-term interest rates were different, past short-term rates might be useful in predicting long-term rates.

The practical implications of this are important. If the Fed adopts a new money management procedure, the time pattern of short-term interest rates will probably vary. If an econometric model had a term-structure equation based on the old regime, it will not specify the correct relationship between long- and short-term rates in the new regime. Thus long-term rates will not be accurately forecast, and consequently, there may be substantial forecasting errors in any sector of a macro model that involves long-term interest rates.

A final example can be taken from investment theory. According to the neoclassical investment model of Dale Jorgenson, the desired capital stock, and hence investment, depends intimately on the cost of capital that is, in essence, equivalent to the rental cost for a unit of capital. This rental cost is affected by interest rates, depreciation, and taxes. The investment tax credit, which allows a corporation to write a fraction of new investment expenditure off its taxes, is potentially an important policy tool for affecting the cost of capital and investment.

Lucas observed that the political environment in which the investment tax credit operated had important implications for measuring the true cost of capital that should be used in econometric models. Imagine two stylized political environments for the investment tax credit. In the first the investment tax credit is enacted rarely but once it is enacted, it remains in force for a while. In the second stylized environment the tax credit is enacted frequently but only remains in effect for short periods of time.

Now consider the cost of capital when an investment tax credit is just enacted. In the second environment the cost of capital will be appreciably lower. The reason is simple: In the second environment the probability of the tax credit disappearing is very high. Investors, in this world, anticipate a high probability of a capital gain on their newly purchased capital equipment. This would occur because the resale value of the undepreciated part of the equipment will be *higher* without the credit because new investors will have to buy machines without the benefit of the credit. The anticipated capital gain from the likely removal of the credit lowers the cost of capital to the firm. Lucas (1976) presents an example to illustrate the quantitative importance of this effect.

In this example it is the policy environment itself that determines the appropriate econometric specification of the investment function. Almost all empirical investment equations simply ignore this issue, and hence may give seriously misleading predictions to the response of investment to investment tax credits.

Is there any way to escape Lucas's conclusion that existing econometric models are worthless for evaluating policy? As long as the scope for policy evaluation is somewhat restricted, econometric models can be useful. Mishkin (1979) argued that most estimated econometric relationships will embody the stochastic relationships of the variables that actually prevailed during the estimation period. As long as simulations can be designed that preserve these relationships, the model can be of some use. More generally, Sims (1980) has argued that many policy actions are really exercises within a stable framework so that equations of econometric models may actually be invariant to some types of policy actions. Major shifts in policy, however, could not be evaluated along these lines – they most likely would not maintain past historical relationships or be explicable within the existing policy canons.

Except for cases in which policy is not really being "changed," Lucas's criticisms go right to the heart of existing econometric practice. Most econometric equations are estimates of *decision rules* that reflect the current economic environment. These decision rules, however, will change when the economic environment changes. Estimated decision rules will only be useful if the policy changes that are contemplated have the same form as those in the past. This means that using the estimated decision rules gives only limited scope for policy evaluation.

There are econometric alternatives. It is possible to estimate econometric models in which expectations are assumed to be rational and which can be used for policy evaluation. To illustrate this point, consider a simple macro model estimated by John Taylor (1979).

Taylor's model consists of two basic equations,

$$y_t = B_0 + B_1 y_{t-1} + B_2 y_{t-2}$$
$$+ B_3(m_t - P_t) + B_4(m_{t-1} - P_{t-1})$$
$$+ B_5 \hat{\pi}_t + B_6 t \tag{3.22}$$

$$\pi_t = \pi_{t-1} + \gamma_1 \hat{y}_t + \gamma_0 \tag{3.23}$$

where y_t is the log of real expenditures measured as a deviation from trend; m_t is the log of nominal money balances during period t, P_t is the log of the price level, π_t is the rate of inflation that is defined as $P_{t+1} - P_t$; and $\hat{\pi}_t$, $\hat{y}_t$ are the expectations of inflation and expenditure, respectively, taken at time $t - 1$, and all stochastic terms have been suppressed. Equation (3.22) is an aggregate demand relationship, whereas equation (3.23) is an aggregate supply relationship.

There are two key assumptions that Taylor makes that are important in understanding the model. First, prices are *predetermined* in any given period, having been set in the previous period. The rationale for this is a story about overlapping labor contracts. Second, the money stock in period t is equal to what actors had anticipated the period before. One explanation for this assumption might be that the monetary authorities follow stable rules that are known by the private sector; in any case there can be no monetary surprises. These two assumptions considerably simplify the econometric analysis and make it possible for the monetary authorities to affect the probability distribution of output.

Equations (3.22) and (3.23) contain two unobservable variables – the expectations of inflation and expenditures. The rational expectations hypothesis is used to eliminate these unobservables. The procedure is simple. First, take the conditional expectations of both sides of the equations. Because the price level and the money stock in time t are assumed to be known as time $t - 1$, this leads to two simultaneous equations that can be solved for $\hat{\pi}_t$ and $\hat{y}_t$. In turn, these can be substituted back into equations (3.22) and (3.23), leading to the equations:

$$y_t = a\{B_0 + B_1 y_{t-1} + B_2 y_{t-2}$$
$$+ B_3(m_t - P_t) + B_4(m_{t-1} - P_{t-1})$$
$$+ B_5 \pi_{t-1} + B_6 t\} \tag{3.24}$$

$$\pi_t = a\{\gamma_1 [B_1 y_{t-1} + B_2 y_{t-2}$$
$$+ B_3(m_t - P_t) + B_4(m_{t-1} - P_{t-1})]$$
$$+ \pi_{t-1} + \gamma_1 B_6 t + \gamma_1 B_0 + \gamma_0\} \qquad (3.25)$$

where $a = 1/(1 - B_5\gamma_1)$. These two equations contain only observable variables and can be estimated.

The model is constructed so that expectations are rational and policy evaluation is possible. With alternative rules for the behavior of the nominal money stock, rules that the private sector knows, equations (3.24) and (3.25) can be used to explore the trade-offs that exist in this model between the variability of real output and inflation. Taylor (1981) later used the model to explore the consequences of gradualist stabilization rules suggested by monetarists.

This model does not completely avoid the problems raised by Lucas. Expectations are rational but the coefficients of the model are assumed to be invariant to changes in policies. It is likely, however, that some of these coefficients would be functions of the variability of output or inflation. The slope of the short-run Phillips curve (the α_1 parameter), in particular, might be endogenous.

An alternative program suggested by Sargent (1981a) is to try to estimate the underlying parameters of preferences and technology. Equipped with utility and production functions, economic theory can be used to predict how people will behave in alternative stochastic environments. This approach places a substantial burden on economic theory, and very restrictive functional forms for cost and utility functions are currently required to even approach tractable models.

The econometric work along these lines is in its infancy. Wallis (1980) and, in particular, Hansen and Sargent (1980) have sketched the theoretical solution to some of the econometric problems. These are very complex procedures and may tax existing computer budgets, if not computer facilities. The principle, however, is simple: We want to estimate parameters that will be invariant to policy changes and not simply estimate the existing decision rules. In this way the effects of alternative policies can be calculated.

It is rare for a critique in economics to affect all elements of a macro model, but Lucas's (1976) critique does just this. Lucas not only argued that a particular theory of consumption or investment was flawed but also stressed that the traditional use of estimated decision rules was incorrect. Any sector of the economy in which expectations figure prominently is necessarily affected. From this brief survey of examples it is difficult to think of an area not subject to his critique.

4

Efficient markets
and rational expectations

The proposition that markets process information efficiently may be controversial for macroeconomic models but has served as the foundation of research in financial markets for some time. The rational expectations hypothesis, under the name of the "efficient markets model," has been used quite extensively in financial market research. The efficient markets model asserts that prices of securities are freely flexible and reflect all available information. In its more formal statements the model asserts that prices are related to conditional expectations.

These ideas have become so familiar to economists that they have even filtered down to the introductory level of instruction in the form of the random walk theory. Price changes, it is alleged, must follow random patterns. If past prices or volume played any role in predicting future price behavior, then Wall Street technicians would soon discover these patterns. As technicians began to act on their findings, prices would adjust so that the pattern disappeared. For example, if it was predicted that stock prices would rise by 10 percent by the end of the week, investors would rush out and purchase securities until their prices rose by 10 percent. Prices would increase at that time rather than at the end of the week. Thus no established patterns calculated from past data can ever be used to predict future price behavior. Price changes, therefore, must be random.

According to some simple versions of the theory, the price of a security today is equal to the conditional expectation of tomorrow's price. The change in the price between today and tomorrow is thus analogous to a forecast error. The orthogonality property of conditional expectations ensures that the forecast error (i.e., the price change) is uncorrelated with any available information. Thus price changes must be unpredictable in this version of the efficient markets hypothesis.

The mechanism by which markets become efficient is usually not treated explicitly in elementary discussions. When considered in depth, the story resembles the one told by Cootner:

> Given the uncertainty of the real world, the many actual and virtual investors will have many, perhaps equally many, price forecasts . . . If any group of investors was consistently better than average in forecasting stock price, they would bring the present price closer to the true value. Conversely, investors who were worse than average in forecasting ability would carry less and less weight. If this process worked well enough, the present price would reflect the best information about the future in the sense that the present price, plus normal profits, would be the best estimate of the future price. (1967:80)

Competition among investors, therefore, ensures that the most accurate information is embodied in prices and that the market functions efficiently.

There have always been a few troubling aspects to this theory in its simplest form. What about the security analysts employed on Wall Street? Does the efficient markets hypothesis necessarily imply that their contributions are worthless? Who ensures that these markets remain efficient and is there an economic reward required for this service?

There have always been some puzzling aspects of stock market behavior. For example, no one has ever really given a convincing explanation why the stock market crashed in 1929. The most plausible stories appear inconsistent with the notion of efficient markets. The popular version of the crash begins with tales of overspeculation in the late 1920s that affected the whole economy, from the Everglades to Wall Street. Somehow the speculative bubble burst and, as paper wealth deteriorated, the economy began its downward spiral into the Great Depression. Was this important episode consistent with the efficient markets hypothesis?

Despite these doubts, the paradigm at first appeared to be robust. As research in the 1960s and early seventies grew more sophisticated in terms of statistical techniques and the maintained hypotheses examined, very few disconfirming pieces of evidence were noted. In spite of some lingering doubts, the evidence seemed to support even very simple versions of the efficient markets hypothesis.

Starting in the mid-1970s, theoretical and empirical work first became more critical of the earlier notions. Economic theorists began both to question the claims of "efficiency" and to investigate the circumstances under which market prices revealed all the information in the economy, even when that information was held by only a subset of market participants. This was something of a paradox. If efficiency required that all available information be aggregated into prices, then why would anyone bother to collect information to begin with? These concerns attracted the attention of some of the best theorists in the profession, giving rise to a challenging literature, which we will term the "microeconomics of rational expectations." The next section discusses these developments, which are essential for evaluating any claims of market efficiency.

Microeconomic theorists did not only begin to express some doubts about efficient markets; within the academic finance community the capital-asset-pricing model, the vehicle for examining the efficient markets hypothesis for individual securities or portfolios, drew some spirited attacks. At the same time, new statistical techniques were developed that seemed to show that stock and bond prices were much too "volatile" to be consistent with traditional efficient market models.

To appreciate these critiques, we should first develop the theoretical foundation for the traditional efficient market models – the martingale and capital-asset-pricing models – and review the early empirical evidence that provided considerable support for these hypotheses. Despite the recent critiques, they remain important tools for analyzing financial markets. We then turn to a critical discussion of the capital-asset-pricing model and to a discussion of the volatility tests and their interpretation. The chapter concludes with an alternative model of market equilibrium that could, in principle, be consistent with both the efficient markets hypothesis and recent empirical evidence.

The microeconomics of rational expectations

Diversity of opinions makes life both frustrating and interesting. This diversity of information or opinions, however, plays almost no role in the macroeconomic discussions of rational expectations. The reason for this is quite simple; macroeconomics has been the study of aggregate relationships and has not focused on individual differences among economic actors. This focus is peculiar to rational expectations macroeconomics as well as to traditional Keynesian and monetarist versions.

As the following hypothetical example shows, taking into account diversity of opinions can bring striking gains in economic efficiency. Consider a medium size economic consulting firm in the highly competitive business of selling forecasts of economic activity. In addition to an econometric model, the head of the company has three economists to aid in developing the forecasts. All three economists have sharply different orientations: the first is a monetarist who follows the monetary data religiously; the second is a Keynesian who looks at tax and spending data; and the third is a follower of Joan Robinson, who believes that the "animal spirits" that rule the economic world are best gauged by developments in the financial markets.

The head of the company notices three facts about the forecasts. First, although each analyst made mistakes, there were no systematic under- or overpredictions. Second, the analysts' forecasts were equally as accurate as measured by the variance of the forecast errors. Finally, their forecasting methods were so diverse that the mistakes that the analysts made were totally uncorrelated with one another.

The company head realized that by averaging the forecasts of the analysts the variance of the forecasts could be reduced. Specifically, if each analyst had a forecast error variance equal to σ^2, then the forecast error variance of the simple average of the forecast would be $\sigma^2/3$, a dramatic improvement in the accuracy of the company's forecasts.

In actual situations the gains from combining different forecasts may not be so great. Forecasters may have systematic biases, and frequently forecasts are very highly and positively correlated. The higher the correlation of the forecasts is, the less scope there is for improving accuracy by pooling. If the forecasts were perfectly correlated, pooling would have no effect. It is an empirical question whether pooling of information leads to significant gains in forecasting.

Stephen Figlewski (1980) provides interesting evidence on this issue from his analysis of individual responses to Joseph Livingston's survey. Figlewski noted that the simple averaging of individual survey responses would, in general, waste information. A better strategy would be to "weight" the diverse opinions so as to provide a forecast that minimized the mean squared error of prediction. Using the Livingston sample and a technique for choosing weights based on a model in the finance literature, Figlewski found that errors in predicting the Consumer Price Index (CPI) could be substantially reduced by optimally combining individual forecasts into an aggregate forecast. In particular, using weights estimated on only part of the sample and forecasting out of sample, the optimal forecasts had a mean squared error that was 40 percent less than the sample mean.

Conventional microeconomic theory does not take into account the potential gains from aggregating information. Consider, for example, the standard model of the pure exchange economy. Agents are described by their preferences over goods and their initial endowments. They submit buy and sell orders, and prices then adjust to eliminate excess demands. When the equilibrium price vector has been determined, trade finally occurs. In equilibrium, prices convey the socially established trade-offs among goods to individuals and determine the value of initial endowments, that is, individuals' budget constraints.

The theory remains fundamentally unchanged when uncertainty is introduced by state-contingent markets. State-contingent markets allow individuals to trade in contracts that are only carried out if certain events (states) occur. These markets allow individuals to deal with uncertainty by trading in a variety of contingent claims. Nonetheless, the same type of equilibrium occurs as in the standard exchange economy. Buy and sell orders are taken and prices adjust until all markets, including those for state-contingent claims, clear. Prices again establish the socially determined trade-offs and budget constraints.

In this model an individual's demand for state-contingent commodities will reflect, among other things, the probability that he attaches to that event occurring. Similarly, the bids of other individuals will also reflect their views of the likelihood of certain events. Market prices will, therefore, embody the probability assessments of all the economic agents in the economy. Presumably, the probability assessments of other individuals would be of interest to a particular individual. Yet the model ignores this factor; economic agents do not alter their probability assessments in light of the information revealed in market prices. Economic actors are assumed, in a sense, to be myopic; in forecasting in an uncertain world they only consider what they bring initially to the market and ignore any potential information that may be communicated through prices. Individuals neglect one of the most important sources of information – the price system.

There is a certain irony in the fact that the conventional microeconomic theory of competitive markets has a blind spot with respect to these informational issues. Not too long ago informational efficiencies were viewed as the great advantage of a competitive market system over a planned system. The great debate between Oscar Lange and Ludwig von Mises resulted in an understanding that an ideal competitive market system essentially "solves" the same problem as an efficient central planner would. As Hayek (1945) stressed, the informational requirements for the central planner would be enormous; the advantage of a decentralized, competitive economy is that the knowledge and skills of each individual need not be communicated to a central planner but can still be employed efficiently. Furthermore, as the philosopher Michael Oakeshott (1962) noted, it is impossible to communicate certain types of information such as a mechanic's feel for the ailments of an old car.

In our modern economy, problems of risk and information have taken on more important roles. Although the idiosyncratic knowledge of the baker, tailor, tinker, and mechanic is still important today, the efforts of investors, brokers, and others in the risk-spreading business are also significant. If standard, competitive market theory cannot fully explicate the role of the latter group, what remains of the informational case for the competitive market system? Could a central planning agency gather and communicate information and improve the efficiency of a market system? Conventional microeconomic models of the competitive system are silent on this point.

Just as the topic of expectations excited macroeconomists in the 1970s, informational issues were at the heart of interesting research in microeconomic theory during the decade. In particular, Sanford Grossman (1976, 1978) and others focused on precisely the issue of market prices revealing information to traders. Both the modeling techniques and results warrant careful examination.

These ideas are best presented in the context of a simple model due to Grossman (1976). There are n types of traders with sufficient numbers of each type to ensure perfect competition. Types of traders are distinguished by the information they are privy to. Specifically, type i traders have access to information denoted Y_i.

There are two assets in the economy, a safe asset and a risky asset whose price in time period 1, P_1, is a random variable. For each trader the price that will prevail in period 1 is linked to his information,

$$Y_i = P_1 + \epsilon_i \tag{4.1}$$

The difference between this information and the actual price for the risky asset, ϵ_i, is a random variable that measures the trader's uncertainty.

In period 0 the economic agents trade among themselves, with each individual maximizing his expected utility of wealth in period 1. An equilibrium price $P_0(Y_1, \ldots, Y_n)$ for the risky asset is established with the notation emphasizing the point that the price for the risky asset will be a function of the information that the agents have.

Consider first a "naive equilibrium" for this system in which individual agents do *not* take into account that market prices reflect other agents' information. In this world each agent will consult his information, Y_i, and his utility function and derive his demand function for the risky asset, $X_i^d(P_0|Y_i)$. The notation indicates that agent i's demand function is conditional only on his information. If the stock of the risky asset is $\overline{X}$, then the "naive equilibrium" condition will be

$$\sum_{i=1}^{n} X_i^d (P_0 \mid Y_i) = \overline{X} \tag{4.2}$$

This determines the market clearing price P_0.

Now suppose this market game is played a number of times and one of the agents keeps track of (Y_i, P_0, P_1); that is, his information, the market clearing price in period 0, and the actual price that prevails for the risky asset in period 1. The agent regresses P_1 on both Y_i and P_0 and finds that the coefficient on P_0 is significant statistically. The agent realizes that this means that the market clearing price conveys *additional* information to him above his own private information source.

Next time the game is played the agent acts naively at first and waits until the market is just about to clear and observes P_0. He then changes his bid in line with his regression equation forecast, altering the market equilibrium price. As long as the market clearing price conveys additional information about the final outcome, agents will have an incentive to keep changing their bids.

What would be an equilibrium for the system when all the agents realize that the market clearing price conveys additional information?

The demand for risky assets can, in this case, be written as $X_i^d(P_0|Y_i,$ $P_0(Y_1, \ldots, Y_n))$, which states that the demand for risky assets is conditioned not just on private information but also on the market clearing price that, in turn, reflects all available information. The equilibrium condition for this case can be written as

$$\sum_{i=1}^{n} X_i^d \left[P_0(Y_1, \ldots, Y_n) \mid Y_i, P_0(Y_1, \ldots, Y_n)\right] = \bar{X} \qquad (4.3)$$

The solution to this problem is a price function in which the market clearing price is a function of the underlying information in the economy.

Grossman (1976) terms this a *rational expectations equilibrium*. Individual agents take into account that both they and other agents have information and that the market price for the risky asset reflects this information. In this equilibrium no individual agent will have an incentive to change his bid at the very last moment.

To study the equilibrium of this problem, Grossman made two assumptions:

    1. Each individual had a utility function that exhibited constant absolute risk aversion.
    2. The ϵ_i were distributed jointly normal and uncorrelated with one another.

With these rather strong assumptions, Grossman was able to prove that an equilibrium existed for the model having the property that the price function $P_0(Y_1, \ldots, Y_n)$ was a *sufficient statistic* for all the information. Or, in other words, the market clearing price summarizes *all* the information available throughout the economy. Each trader would find his own information to be redundant.

This is a rather remarkable result. In a rational expectations equilibrium one price conveys all the information available for forecasting P_1 even though there are n different sources of information. This single price summarizes all that agents need to know and reveals it to the traders.

In subsequent work Grossman (1978) was able to obtain the same results for a set of risky assets but with much weaker assumptions. As long as the quantity demanded of risky assets in aggregate increased as their price decreased, and the information and asset returns were jointly normal, then market prices will reveal all the information to traders. In this paper Grossman developed the useful notion of an *artificial economy*, one in which each trader had access to all the information. He then showed that an equilibrium existed in which prices were sufficient statistics in the artificial economy if and only if they were sufficient statistics in the basic (nonartificial) economy. The proof was completed by showing that his assumptions ensured that prices were sufficient statistics for the artificial economy. Prices, therefore, were perfect aggregators of information – all the information in the economy is communicated to each trader through the price system.

With this result it is possible to state a strong welfare proposition. Imagine a central planner who had all the information available in the economy. A rational expectations equilibrium in which prices reveal information cannot be dominated by the planner in the Pareto sense; it is not possible to raise the expected utility of one individual without making someone else worse off. This means that there is no advantage to collecting information centrally; an equilibrium in which prices convey information makes this unnecessary.

Grossman went on to suggest that this equilibrium is somewhat unrealistic. If the price system conveyed everything to the traders, there would be little incentive to collect information. To make this point more concretely, assume that there are only two types of traders, informed and uninformed, and costs for gathering the information that is necessary to become informed. Consider an equilibrium in which only some of the traders are informed. If market prices reveal the information to the uninformed, they get the benefits of the information without incurring the costs of obtaining it. However, the informed traders would not be satisfied with this state of affairs – they will no longer collect the information because it brings them no additional edge. However, if no one collects the information, then an incentive emerges for someone to begin doing so. An equilibrium does not exist for this model; some individuals will always want to change their decision about gathering information.

Grossman and Stiglitz (1976:247–8) expressed this point precisely, "If markets are perfectly arbitraged all the time, there are never any profits to be made from the activity of arbitrage. But then, how do arbitragers make money, particularly if there are costs associated with obtaining information about whether markets are already perfectly arbitraged?'' One of the more interesting resolutions to this problem has been offered by Grossman and Stiglitz (1980) themselves.

They develop a model in which identical individuals have an option of purchasing information about the return on a risky asset. Uninformed traders cannot, however, obtain this information through simply observing the market price, because there is an additional source of uncertainty in the model – the supply of risky assets – so that, for uninformed traders, the price is a "noisy" signal. Prices no longer simply convey the information of informed traders; they also reflect the uncertain supply of the stock of the risky asset.

Traders decide whether to become informed based on the expected utility of informed versus uninformed traders. In equilibrium a trader is indifferent between being informed and uninformed. Informed traders outperform the uninformed traders in the market but also have to pay for the cost of acquiring information. Some of this information is communicated to the uninformed traders but the price signal is noisy and informed traders thus maintain a competitive edge.

The higher the proportion of informed traders, the more information market prices convey about the return on the risky asset. As more individuals become informed, however, the expected utility of informed traders falls because they communicate more information to the uninformed traders and consequently lose their competitive advantage. In equilibrium both the number of informed traders and the "informativeness" of the price system are simultaneously determined. The price system, however, will never be totally informative – that would destroy the incentive to gather information. If efficient markets theory requires that the price system be totally informative, then, Grossman and Stiglitz argued, it is not a coherent doctrine. But their aim was "to redefine the Efficient Markets notion, not destroy it" (1980:404).

There has been other work on this topic. Bray (1981) developed a model in which individuals are both producers and speculators and have information about both market demands and their own supply. In general, the market price will not communicate all available information to the traders. Information about the demand side of the market interferes with information from the supply side and prevents the market price from summarizing all the information. This is similar to the Grossman–Stiglitz device of introducing noise into the system to prevent markets from revealing too much.

Radner (1979) examined the question of the existence of a rational expectations equilibrium when the number of alternative states (i.e., alternative outcomes) is finite. He established that, in a technical sense, rational expectations equilibria will "almost always" exist – circumstances under which an equilibrium may fail to exist can be considered negligible. In addition, when rational expectations equilibrium do exist, they will reveal all the information. Radner's paper, although very general in some respects, differs from the other work in the literature by allowing for only a finite set of alternative outcomes.

Work by Allen (1981) relaxed this assumption of finiteness and proved a result that, in a sense, summarized the earlier findings in this literature. She showed that a rational expectations equilibrium that reveals all information will almost always exist if there are more prices and markets in the economy than there are types of uncertainties (e.g., demand and supply) that can affect agents. The Grossman–Stiglitz (1980) work illustrates this theorem: Introducing noise into a model with other uncertainty and only one price was sufficient to prevent the price from revealing all the available information.

Although the microeconomic literature on rational expectations has challenged some of the claims of the efficient markets literature, the basic insights of the efficient markets literature still remain. For example, no models of rational expectations equilibria ever suggest that costless information could be used to make a profit in a financial market. Furthermore, the literature demonstrates how it is possible to construct models in which incentives for information gathering remain without any trader being able to earn excess profits. This depends on having "few enough" markets relative to types of uncertainty. Finally, the provocative work already completed suggests that the efficient markets notion is a useful and productive research paradigm.

Efficient markets: theory and early tests

Early empirical investigations into the behavior of prices in financial markets revealed that price behavior could be described as a random walk. Prices are said to follow a random walk if price changes are random and independently distributed. The work of Kendall (1953), in particular, demonstrated this for a wide variety of markets in commodities and stocks. Kendall was pleased by his results but thought that some economists would be disturbed by his findings.

> To the statistician there is some pleasure in the thought that the symmetrical distribution reared its graceful head undisturbed amid the uproar of the Chicago wheat-pit. The economist, I suspect, or at any rate the trade cyclist, will look for statistical snags before he is convinced of the absence of systematic movements. (1953:13)

As Fama (1970) describes, some economists, including Alexander and Cootner, argued that the approximate random walks of security prices were outcomes of an ideal competitive market. Both thought that this evidence indicated the market was processing new information efficiently but neither offered a formal theory linking market efficiency with the stochastic properties of price series. Samuelson (1965) was the first to formulate a rigorous theory of efficient markets.

Samuelson noted that the embryonic efficient markets literature appeared to be making claims that were not necessarily true. For example, Kendall found that spot prices (i.e., current market prices) for wheat followed a random walk. Samuelson thought that this was by no means a necessary outcome – it is easy to imagine a run of good weather producing a series of good crops, thereby depressing prices for several periods in a row. In more technical terms, serial correlation in the weather could easily induce serial correlation in grain supplies and prices. Samuelson did, however, think that the efficient markets literature had highlighted an important phenomenon and set out to clarify it. In particular, Samuelson proved that under certain assumptions *futures prices* for commodities would exhibit the properties of a random walk.

Samuelson's proof rests on one fundamental property of conditional expectations. This property can be illustrated with a simple example. Imagine at time t an individual forecasts the price of a stock, P_T, several days ahead in the future, and his forecast is the conditional expectation of the price:

$$\text{today's forecast} = E[P_T | I_t] \qquad T > t \qquad (4.4)$$

The very next day he is again called upon to make another forecast of the price, which also is his conditional expectation:

$$\text{tomorrow's forecast} = E[P_T | I_{t+1}] \qquad T > t + 1 \qquad (4.5)$$

At time t the forecast that he will make tomorrow is a random variable because new information will be available between today and tomorrow. Because these forecasts are conditional expectations they have the following property: *Today's expectation of tomorrow's forecast equals today's forecast*, or symbolically,

$$E\{E[P_T | I_{t+1}] I_t\} = E[P_T | I_t] \qquad (4.6)$$

Intuitively, although new information will be available tomorrow to improve the forecast, the best guess of what that information will be is already embodied in today's forecast. Thus today's best guess of tomorrow's forecast is simply today's forecast. This property of conditional expectations is discussed in Shiller (1978) and Samuelson (1965).

Samuelson based his proof that futures prices fluctuate randomly on this mathematical relation. The key assumption he makes is that the market sets futures prices equal to the conditional expectation of the spot price at the closing date of the contract. Letting $F(t, T)$ stand for the price, at time t, for future delivery of a commodity at time T, one can express this assumption as

$$F(t, T) = E[P_T | I_t] \qquad (4.7)$$

Similarly, tomorrow's price $F(t + 1, T)$ is

$$F(t + 1, T) = E[P_T | I_{t+1}] \qquad (4.8)$$

Samuelson proves that the expected gain from holding a futures contract from period t to period $t + 1$ is zero:

$$E[F(t + 1, T) - F(t, T) \mid I_t] = 0 \qquad (4.9)$$

The gain from holding a contract one day is $F(t + 1, T) - F(t, T)$; the theorem says that the expected gain from holding the contract is zero. This implies that futures prices have the martingale or "fair-game" property.

The proof is an immediate application of the property of conditional expectations previously outlined. Substituting the expressions for the futures prices into equation (4.6) yields

$$E[F(t + 1, T) \mid I_t] = F(t, T)$$

or

$$E[F(t + 1, T) - F(t, T) \mid I_t] = 0 \qquad (4.10)$$

Essentially, today's forecast already embodies the best guess as to what tomorrow's forecast will be so expected profits cannot be made on the change in price.

Samuelson also demonstrated that his model can be extended to include the possibility of speculators earning a constant risk premium for holding futures contracts. In this case, speculators in futures will simply earn, on average, this risk premium for their activity. A positive risk premium implies that there will be an upward drift in the futures price over the course of the contract, a phenomenon known in the futures market literature as "normal backwardation."

Of course, the key to this result is the assumption that futures prices are conditional expectations of future spot prices. Although this may be a plausible assumption, it posed further questions for Samuelson (1965:789–90), "I have not asked where the basic probability distributions are supposed to come from. In whose mind are they *ex ante*? Is there any *ex post* validation of them? Are they supposed to belong to the market as a whole?"

Although Samuelson was one of the earliest theoreticians of the efficient markets theory, it was Eugene Fama (1970, 1976) who combined theory and empirical evidence to make a persuasive case for the efficient markets hypothesis. The finance literature has taken the lead in applying rigorous tests to propositions concerning market efficiency and the conditions that are necessary to test them.

Fama (1976) outlined a view of the efficient markets model and the prerequisites for testing it, which is widely accepted. The basic hypothesis of market efficiency is that financial markets use the true conditional probability distribution in the determination of prices. If $f^m(P_t \mid I_{t-1})$ is the market's probability distribution for future prices that are conditioned on the information set I_{t-1} and $f(P_t \mid I_{t-1})$ is the true conditional distribution, then the theory asserts

$$f^m(P_t \mid I_{t-1}) = f(P_t \mid I_{t-1}) \tag{4.11}$$

This hypothesis, by itself, is untestable. To test the theory, one needs two other hypotheses: (1) The information set must be specified. (2) A model of price determination or market equilibrium must be formulated.

Fama (1970) proposed a convenient, and widely used, classification of the different assumptions about information sets. "Weak-form" tests use an information set that includes just past prices. "Semistrong form" tests augment the information on past prices with any other publicly available information. Finally, "strong-form" tests include information held only by a subset of the market as well as all publicly available information.

From the previous discussion of the microeconomics of efficient markets it is clear that "strong-form" tests may well fail even if markets are "efficient." When information is costly, incentives must remain for individuals to gather it. If "strong-form" or insider information is available only at some costs, it is not evident that the failure of strong-form tests is indicative of market inefficiency.

In addition to specifying the information set, a model of market equilibrium is required to test propositions about efficient markets. To date, all models of market equilibrium (asset price determination) have been cast in terms of expected return. There have been three basic models of expected returns that are employed in the literature: Expected returns are positive, expected returns are constant, and expected returns follow a two-parameter asset pricing model. Each model of expected returns suggests different efficiency tests, which deserve consideration. For all the models the return on an asset, Z_t, is defined as

$$Z_t = \frac{D_t + P_t - P_{t-1}}{P_{t-1}} \qquad (4.12)$$

where

D_t = sum of all dividend or coupon payments received between time $t - 1$ and time t

P_t = price of the security at time t

In other words, the return on an asset is the dividend yield plus capital gains.

Expected returns are positive

The first and simplest model of market equilibrium states that asset prices are always set so that expected returns on all assets are positive or $E(Z_t) > 0$. Expectations are taken with respect to the true conditional probability distribution, given the information set. The expected returns for assets may vary from time to time or asset to asset, but they are hypothesized to be positive in each period. Although it may seem natural for individuals to require a positive return on all securities, there are some cases (e.g., insurance contracts) in which they may derive a negative expected return. In any case, the hypothesis of positive expected returns has strong testable implications.

If expected returns are always positive, a buy-and-hold strategy for a security will dominate any strategy that dictates selling short or not holding the security for any length of time. As long as expected returns are always positive, not holding a security means sacrificing expected return whereas short selling is essentially a gamble that the expected return will not be positive. Thus the joint hypothesis of efficient markets and positive expected returns can be rejected if a strategy exists that involves short selling or not holding a security and produces consistently greater returns than buy-and-hold strategies do.

Perhaps the best known tests along these lines were conducted by Alexander (1964), who examined "filter" strategies for securities. A "y-percent filter" strategy involves buying and holding a security if the price goes up by y percent and short selling if the price falls by y percent. By iterating over the size of the filter, one can choose the rule that maximizes returns. After extensive testing, Alexander concluded that any potential gains from such a strategy would be eliminated by brokers' charges and fees. Although small profits can be produced by small filters, they would involve such frequent trading that even floor traders would find that transactions costs would eliminate any economic profits.

Expected returns are constant

A model of equilibrium that is used extensively in the efficient market literature assumes that the expected return from holding securities is constant over time. If the expected return on a security is constant, then any serial correlation in past data on returns is an indication of market failure. The hypothesis that expected returns are constant can be written as

$$E[\tilde{Z}_t - \bar{Z} \mid I_{t-1}] = 0 \tag{4.13}$$

where

$\bar{Z}$ = constant expected return
$\tilde{Z}_t$ = actual return

The orthogonality property of conditional expectations, discussed in Chapter 1, requires that the difference between actual and expected returns be uncorrelated with any past information; if this were not the case, it would be possible to exploit past information to earn economic profits.

One test of this model is to examine if past returns on equities are correlated with current returns. This involves estimating sample autocorrelations for security returns. Fama (1976) reported sample autocorrelations for a variety of securities and found that they were close to zero. In any sample, it will generally be true that an investigator will find some evidence of nonzero autocorrelations;

however, the bulk of the evidence suggests that these autocorrelations were not very large.

It is important to stress that finding some evidence of significant autocorrelations does not mean that markets are not efficient. In all cases, a joint hypothesis of market efficiency and constant expected returns is being examined. Any autocorrelation in equilibrium, expected returns, would generally lead to some observed autocorrelation in actual returns but would not necessarily indicate that excess profits could be earned.

In testing market efficiency with daily returns on securities, one finds that assumptions about equilibrium returns are not critical. It is generally argued that changes in the equilibrium return for stocks or long-term bonds on a daily basis are only a small part of the actual changes in price. Most price changes for these securities are attributed to the arrival of new information in the market. Autocorrelation tests, therefore, should be relatively powerful for these securities.

Autocorrelation tests are not useful testing for market efficiency for all securities. For example, nominal returns on ninety-day Treasury bills are serially correlated but there is no necessary presumption that this implies market inefficiencies. As Mishkin (1978) and others have pointed out, if typical holding periods are a full three months, then the one-period return on a ninety-day Treasury bill is just the rate on the security itself. Changes in the rate from holding period to holding period, therefore, only reflect changes in expected returns. If expected returns are serially correlated, then rates on these securities will also be serially correlated. The equilibrium model of a constant expected return is clearly not appropriate for short-term government securities that are held to maturity, and serial correlation of returns on these securities does not imply that markets are inefficient.

Further evidence on efficient bond markets is provided by Mishkin (1978, 1981b). In these tests Mishkin assumed that the equilibrium holding return on long-term bonds, R_t, could be described by the sum of the short-term interest rate known at the beginning of the period and a constant liquidity premium. Mishkin (1978) conducted orthogonality tests, exploring if past information could predict excess returns. After correcting for heteroskedasticity, he found very little significant evidence of any market inefficiencies, although some tests (Mishkin 1978:736) were close to indicating that past information was of some use. On the whole, however, the evidence for market efficiency was fairly persuasive.

In other work, Mishkin (1981b) tested whether information on the past history of short-term interest rates and inflation rates was used efficiently in the market for long-term bonds. The tests involved examining whether the stochastic processes that bond market participants believed these variables to follow was the same as the true stochastic processes for the variables. Letting $R_t - R^*$ denote the excess return on long-term bonds, Mishkin argued that the excess return could be expressed as a function of the unanticipated change $(X_t - X_t^\epsilon)$ in a variable (say, the inflation rate), plus a random error term, ϵ_t:

$$R_t - R_t^* = (X_t - X_t^\epsilon)\,\alpha + \epsilon_t \tag{4.14}$$

Assume that the stochastic process for X_t can be written as

$$X_t = \sum_{i=1}^{n} b_i X_{t-1} + \eta_t \tag{4.15}$$

then its expectation, X_t^ϵ, will be

$$X_t^\epsilon = \sum_{i=1}^{n} b_i X_{t-1} \tag{4.16}$$

Substituting equation (4.16) into equation (4.14) gives the observable equation,

$$R_t - R_t^* = (X_t - \sum_{i=1}^{n} b_i X_{t-1})\,\alpha + \epsilon_t \tag{4.17}$$

Equations (4.17) and (4.15) can be estimated jointly and the cross-equation restrictions between the two relations can be tested by standard likelihood ratio tests.

Mishkin's results are intriguing. He found that information about short-term interest rates was used efficiently in the long-term bond market but that information about inflation over the period 1959–69 was not used efficiently. Mishkin argued that this was an unusual historical period, with inflation starting at a low level and persistently rising. The bond market participants, however, were implicitly predicting inflation to recede and return to past trends, which led to the rejection of the rationality tests. Was this period really "unusual" or simply a period when market participants were not up to par? To the extent that it truly was a transition to a new regime, failures of "rationality" tests may be expected; if these transitions are too frequent, then the rationality paradigm will have only limited value.

The hypothesis that expectations are rational and expected returns are constant received surprising support from a study of the market for government securities by Fama (1975). Fama conjectured that expected real returns on Treasury bills were constant and that movements in nominal interest rates reflected expectations of inflation, which, in turn, were formed rationally. These joint hypotheses have two striking implications:

1. Ex post real rates of return should exhibit no significant autocorrelation.
2. Past inflation rates should add no explanatory power to a regression of current inflation on the interest rate prevailing at the beginning of the period.

The first implication follows directly from the assumption of constant expected returns and no arbitrage profits. The second implication is a consequence of the assumption that current interest rates embody the optimal forecast for inflation in his hypothesis.

Using monthly data from 1953 to 1971, Fama (1975) found considerable support for his hypothesis. This created a controversy, for it was commonly believed that interest rates did not simply mirror expected inflation point for point and that monetary policy had had an effect on ex ante real rates during this period. Nelson and Schwert (1977) argued that Fama's tests were not very powerful for testing the hypothesis that real rates were constant ex ante. The essential problem was that mistakes in predicting inflation are probably much larger than movements in anticipated real rates. Under these circumstances, Fama's tests do not have high statistical power.

More recent work over longer sample periods fails to confirm Fama's initial findings. Mishkin (1981c), for example, found systematic variation in the real rate of interest when the sample is extended through the seventies and during the interwar period. These results suggest that Fama's initial findings were peculiar to his sample period during which movements in ex ante real rates of interest were probably small.

Fama's findings raised the question of whether the Federal Reserve could control real interest rates for any extended period of time. As Shiller (1980) pointed out, certain historical episodes, including the pegging of interest rates from World War II to the Fed–Treasury Accord, suggest that real interest rates can be controlled. Shiller, however, also turned up some evidence that is close to the spirit of Fama's model. After the Federal Reserve System was founded, the seasonality in nominal interest rates was reduced as the supply of credit was allowed to respond to seasonal demands. Shiller, however, found little evidence to suggest that the seasonal patterns of real interest rates were affected. It may have been the case that during this period (1914–30), changes in the money stock translated quickly into movements in price levels so that real interest rates were unaffected by monetary policy. The time interval over which the Fed can control real interest rates is still an unresolved question.

Two-parameter models

The two previous models of equilibrium returns were developed for pricing a single security – they had nothing to say about the relative prices of securities or how portfolios of securities should be priced. The finance literature has developed extremely interesting models of relative asset prices, known under the general name of capital-asset-pricing models (CAPM). They have served as the basis for testing efficiency propositions in a world with risky assets.

The CAPM was developed independently by Sharpe (1964), Lintner (1965), and Mossin (1966). The earliest version was based on very strong assumptions:

1. Risk-averse investors choose portfolios based only on single period means and variances of returns.

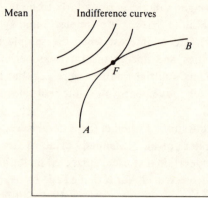

Standard deviation

Figure 4.1 The efficient frontier.

2. There is unlimited borrowing and lending at a riskless rate of interest r and no restrictions on short selling.
3. There are homogeneous expectations.
4. Markets are frictionless, competitive, and all assets are perfectly divisible.

With these assumptions, it is possible to show that expected returns on assets must follow the relation

$$E(R_j) = r + [E(R_M) - r]\beta_j \qquad (4.18)$$

where

$E(R_j)$ = expected return on the jth asset
r = riskless rate of interest
$E(R_M)$ = the expected return on a market portfolio that includes *all* assets weighted by their market values.
$$\beta_j = \frac{\text{covariance } (R_j, R_M)}{\text{variance } (R_M)}$$

Although a complete derivation of the CAPM would lead too far afield, a simple graph can illustrate some of the logic underlying the model. For a fixed set of risky securities it is possible to find portfolios that provide an efficient trade-off between risk and expected return. In Figure 4.1 the curved line *AB* is known as the efficient

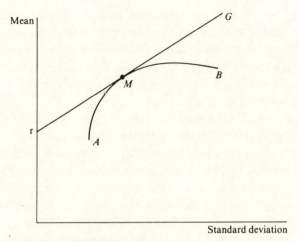

Figure 4.2   The introduction of a riskless asset.

frontier and contains portfolios with maximum expected return for a given level of risk. The frontier is drawn for a given level of initial wealth. The indifference curves in the figure portray the individual's preferences for risk versus return. The portfolio of securities at F is the best choice for this particular individual.

Suppose now that there are a riskless asset and unlimited borrowing and lending opportunities at the interest rate r. As illustrated in Figure 4.2, this leads to an efficient frontier rG, which is a straight line that originates from r and is tangent to the efficient frontier at M. Any portfolio on the efficient frontier consists of a position in the riskless asset (either borrowing or lending) and a portfolio of risky assets, with the proportions of each risky asset the same as in portfolio M. Therefore, every investor who holds any risky securities will want to hold them in the same proportions. Sharpe (1964) and others observed that portfolio M must be the market portfolio, that is, the portfolio consisting of all the securities. Thus every investor takes a position in riskless assets and the market portfolio.

It is not difficult to show that this basic economic logic leads to equation (4.18), which is known as the security market line. The intuition behind this equation is straightforward. The term β_j, known as the "beta" of the security, measures how the return on the security is related to the market. The higher the beta is, the more likely that the return on the security will move with the market. Assets with high betas are more risky because their riskiness cannot be eliminated by holding a diversified portfolio – their returns are highly correlated with the market.

Indeed, the basic CAPM equation implies that a security will only earn an expected return that exceeds the riskless rate of interest to the extent that the return on the security is correlated with the return on the market. In an efficient capital market, fluctuations in security returns that are not correlated with the market can be diversified away by holding a sufficient number of assets, and the market pays no premium for risk that can be diversified away. The market does, however, pay a premium for undiversifiable risk; this premium is the beta of the security times the "market price of risk," measured by the difference between the expected return on the market portfolio and the riskless rate.

There has been extensive testing of various versions of the CAPM. Black et al. (1972) found that although the Sharpe–Lintner–Mossin model fit the data reasonably well, there were some empirical anomalies. High-beta securities appeared to earn lower yields than those predicted by the theory, whereas low-beta securities earned higher yields. Moreover, the slope of the risk-return line, although close to linearity, as predicted by the theory, exhibited considerable variation over subperiods in the sample. Clearly, some modification of the theory was needed.

Black (1972) showed that many of these empirical anomalies could be accounted for by a model that relaxed just one of the assumptions of the earlier asset pricing models. He demonstrated that with no opportunities for riskless borrowing or lending, expected returns would be given by

$$E(R_j) = E(R_{z0}) + [E(R_m) - E(R_{z0})]\beta_j \qquad (4.19)$$

where $E(R_{z0})$ is the expected return on a minimum variance portfolio of securities that is uncorrelated with the market portfolio.

This model differs from the previous one only in that the riskless rate is replaced by the expected return on the minimum variance "zero-beta" portfolio–a portfolio of securities that is uncorrelated with the market portfolio. The minimum variance zero-beta portfolio plays the role of the riskless asset when borrowing and lending opportunities in riskless assets are absent. Because the expected return on the zero-beta portfolio can vary from period to period, it can account for the variation in the slope of the risk–return line, as well as for what appeared to be the undervaluation of risk in the market.

The rational expectations hypothesis plays an important role in these tests. Most statements of the theory are in terms of individuals' beliefs concerning the means and variances of individual securities. To test these models, one must identify these subjective beliefs. The rational expectations hypothesis provides the solution to this problem by equating the subjective beliefs of individuals with the actual means and variances of securities that prevailed during the period.

Jensen (1979) provided a careful review of the existing tests of this "two-factor" model. These tests included examining whether the risk–return line was truly linear and whether the market rewarded only nondiversifiable risk. The results of these tests generally conform to the theory. As Jensen (1979:37) summarized the evidence, "the major characteristics of the process generating asset returns seems to be well described by the two factor model." This brief summary of the two-parameter model understates the immense amount of theoretical and empirical work undertaken within this framework. But this process of scientific examination led to some doubts concerning the validity of the model.

Against the paradigm

Considerable research within the academic finance community has been conducted to evaluate various aspects of the efficient market hypothesis, so it is not surprising that the first doubts about some of the models originated within this group. The two-parameter model, the explicit theory of risk-premium determination, first came under attack. In a spirited critique of the capital-asset-pricing model, Richard Roll (1977) raised some concerns over the previous tests of the model and expressed skepticism over the future tests of the model.

Roll argued that many of the tests of the CAPM were not really "tests" at all; in a sense, previous investigators had examined properties that were very close to logical or mathematical properties of the data themselves. To understand Roll's critique, one should recall the notion of an efficient portfolio. An efficient portfolio is a collection of securities that, for a given level of risk, yields the highest possible return. Given a collection of securities, it is always possible to find the set of portfolios that are efficient ex post. Roll showed that these ex post efficient portfolios possess certain properties.

Specifically, consider a portfolio that is mean-variance efficient ex post (call it M). Roll proved two propositions concerning these portfolios.

1. There exists another portfolio of securities, Z, such that Z and M are uncorrelated.
2. For any security j, the return on security j, r_j, can be expressed as

$$r_j = r_z + \beta_j[r_m - r_z] \qquad (4.20)$$

where

$$r_z = \text{return on portfolio } Z$$
$$r_m = \text{return on portfolio } M$$
$$\beta_j = \frac{\text{covariance } (r_j, r_m)}{\text{variance } (r_m)}$$

These two propositions have important implications for testing the CAPM. As Roll argued, there is really only one testable implication of the model – namely, the market portfolio is mean-variance efficient. If the market portfolio is efficient, Roll's second proposition implies that the Black (1972) version of the security market line *must* hold in the sample. Finding that the security market line is linear or that other factors do not explain security returns provides no additional confirmation of the hypothesis – these facts are implied by the mean-variance efficiency of the market portfolio.

Roll's first point, therefore, was that there is really only one basic proposition to test. If the market portfolio is mean-variance efficient, returns on individual securities must be explicable by the security market line of the Black (1972) model.

Roll's second point concerned the use of proxies for the market portfolio. Most studies used, for example, stocks listed on the New York Stock Exchange, but Roll insisted that this was a very narrow definition of the market portfolio. A true ''market portfolio'' would include claims on real estate, human capital, and other nonmarketable assets. Traded stocks form only a subset of the true market.

The issue of proxies for the market portfolio is important because the tests of the models hinge on whether the market portfolio is efficient. There are two basic mistakes that can be made in this regard. (1) The proxy portfolio could be efficient, but the true market portfolio may not be. This would lead to falsely accepting the model. (2) The proxy may be inefficient, but the true market portfolio could be efficient. This would lead to incorrectly rejecting the model. Roll discussed in some detail the actual tests conducted on the CAPM and argued that they shed little light on the validity of the model.

Of course, all economic models use proxies in one form or another and, if one insists on perfect data, few theories could be tested. Roll, however, argued that in this case the problem was worse than usual. Mean-variance efficiency of the market portfolio is the *only* testable implication of the theory; the tests with security market lines will necessarily hold if the market portfolio is efficient. Because there is only one testable implication, the lack of complete data is a severe problem. Thus the future or potential testability of the model is also in question.

Aside from raising some problems with existing tests of the two-parameter model, Roll's paper also crystallized the ever present doubts about the model. There were always skeptics who were ready to attack the model because its assumptions (frictionless markets, homogeneous expectations, etc.) were so strong. A visible sign of the increased skepticism was a symposium in the *Journal of Financial Economics* (1978) that was devoted to exploring pieces of evidence that were inconsistent with the traditional models of efficiency and market equilibrium.

Ball's (1978) study, which surveyed existing evidence of the reaction of stock prices to earnings announcements, is an example of this work. The persistence of excess returns on securities during the postannouncement period was a consistent finding across the studies surveyed. According to efficient markets theory, prices should adjust to eliminate the potential for earning excess returns. The evidence suggests, however, that excess returns (as measured by two-parameter models) were available on securities that had favorable earnings announcements.

Ball also described a related finding that other publicly available information could aid in earning excess returns. The best known example of this is the Value Line rating system, which has been shown to predict stocks that earn excess returns. Ball argued that this evidence of market inefficiency is most likely an indictment of the two-parameter model rather than an indication of market inefficiency.

This evidence is not necessarily definitive. For example, Watts (1978), in a careful examination of the issue, still found evidence of excess returns during postearnings announcement periods. However, the violation of efficiency only occurred during one subperiod and only brokers could have profited from the information. The accumulation of bits of disconfirming evidence, however, is impressive. As Jensen (1978:95), the editor of the Symposium, wrote, "viewed as a whole, these pieces of evidence begin to stack up in a manner which make a much stronger case for the necessity to carefully review both our acceptance of the efficient market theory and our methodological procedures."

A similar intellectual pattern emerged in the literature in international finance. To show that floating exchange rates are conducive to economic stability, many investigators such as Frenkel (1977) examined the "efficiency" of foreign exchange markets. One of the areas they examined was whether the forward market for foreign exchange was efficient. According to the generally accepted theory, an efficient forward market for foreign exchange required that the forward rate be an unbiased predictor of future spot rates. The reason for this requirement is easy to understand. A forward contract for foreign exchange is a contract to deliver foreign exchange at a specified future date at a currently determined price. If the price in the forward market is not an unbiased predictor of the subsequent spot rate, it would be possible to earn economic profits by taking an appropriate position in the forward market. It should be noted that unbiasedness is only a necessary condition for market efficiency in this model; a more stringent requirement of market efficiency is that the difference between the forward rate and subsequent spot rate should be unpredictable, using information available at the time of the initial contract. Furthermore, there is obviously a joint hypothesis being tested – market efficiency combined with the hypothesis that expected returns are constant over time and equal to zero.

The early evidence [e.g., Frenkel (1977)] was consistent with this strong version of market efficiency. Later work, for example, by Hansen and Hodrick (1980) indicated that this hypothesis was not literally true. Using techniques and data designed to increase the statistical power of their tests, they found that, for several currencies, past forecast errors helped to predict current forecast errors, which violated the orthogonality principle. Similar evidence was presented that rejected rationality for the French franc during the 1920s.

Hansen and Hodrick emphasized that they were testing a joint hypothesis involving efficient use of information along with a particular model of market equilibrium. They indicated the need to provide alternative models of market equilibrium that would be consistent with their empirical results and the rational expectations hypothesis.

The most interesting of the new wave of attacks on the efficient markets model is based on "volatility" tests that were originally developed by LeRoy and Porter (1981) and Shiller (1981a). This rapidly growing literature has been applied to markets for bonds, stocks, and foreign exchange and has been the subject of a recent survey article by Shiller (1981b). These "volatility" tests have been extremely provocative because they have generally pointed to market inefficiencies, whereas traditional tests (orthogonality tests) have not detected these inefficiencies.

Volatility tests rest on a simple premise – forecasts based on conditional expectations should have lower variances (i.e., be less volatile) than actual outcomes. Consider, for example, forecasting the outcome for each period of the following experiment. A computer generates a random number from a normal distribution with a mean of zero and a variance of σ^2. The drawings are independent and always made from the same distribution. Clearly, for each period the best forecast is the same – namely, zero. The variance of the optimal forecast will be zero. The variance of the actual outcome, however, will be the variance of the distribution (σ^2), which exceeds the variance of the optimal forecast.

More generally, let P_t^* be the variable to be forecast. Then the optimal forecast is given by

$$P_t = E[P_t^* \mid I_{t-1}] \tag{4.21}$$

Let u_t denote the forecast error, which, by the orthogonality principle, must be uncorrelated with the forecast P_t. Thus $P_t^* = P_t + u_t$ and, taking the variance of both sides,

$$\text{var}(P_t^*) = \text{var}(P_t) + \text{var}(u_t)$$

or

$$\text{var}(P_t^*) \geq \text{var}(P_t) \qquad \text{since } \text{var}(u_t) \geq 0 \tag{4.22}$$

This rather trivial fact about conditional expectation forecasts is important because most popular theories of long-term bond and stock prices claim that prices of these securities are forecasts. Concentrating on stock prices, recall that the most basic theory states that stock prices, P_t, are equal to the discounted present value of expected future dividends, or

$$P_t = \sum_{k=0}^{\infty} \left(\frac{1}{1+r}\right)^{k+1} E_t \, d_{t+k} \tag{4.23}$$

where

$$r \qquad = \text{ constant discount rate}$$

$E_t d_{t+k}$ = expected value at time t of dividends paid at time $t + k$

Let P_t^* stand for the ex post or perfect foresight discounted stream of future dividends:

$$P_t^* = \sum_{k=0}^{\infty} \left(\frac{1}{1 + r}\right)^{k+1} d_{t+k} \qquad (4.24)$$

This is the price an individual would pay if he knew what the actual stream of future dividends would be.

The traditional theory of stock price determination can be stated succinctly as

$$P_t \qquad = \qquad E[P_t^* \mid I_t] \qquad (4.25)$$

actual stock price = conditional expectation of future dividends

This symbolism makes it evident that stock prices are essentially forecasts.

Because stock prices are forecasts, they should be less volatile than the ex post justified price or the price that someone with perfect foresight would pay for stocks. However, just the opposite is true. Stock prices are much too volatile to be explained by changes in dividends. The variance of actual prices greatly exceeds the variance of the actual discounted stream of future dividends, clearly violating the "volatility" principle that forecasts should be less volatile than the variables to be forecasted.

Common experience suggests that stock prices are too volatile to be explained by changes in dividends. The meanderings of the stock market are well documented and the source of much speculation, yet when a firm fails to meet its dividend payments, it becomes a major news item. The "volatility" literature goes beyond this casual level of observation and formulates restrictions on the variance of stock prices based on the time-series patterns for dividends. The same basic techniques have been employed to explore long-term bond prices in relation to short-term interest rates and exchange rates in relation to money growth rate differentials. The results of these tests indicate that asset prices are too volatile to be described simply as forecasts of their underlying determinants.

Some additional insight can be gained by examining equivalent expressions for the stock market pricing equation. After some manipulation, Equation (4.23) can be written as

$$E_t\left\{ \frac{P_{t+1} - P_t}{P_t} + \frac{d_t}{P_t} \right\} = r \qquad (4.26)$$

$$\underset{\text{expected capital gain}}{} + \underset{\text{dividend yield}}{} = \underset{\text{interest rate}}{}$$

This equation implies that the price of securities adjusts so that the dividend yield plus expected capital gains, which together comprise the return to holding the security, equal the prevailing interest rate. Further manipulation leads to the expression

$$E_t\{P_{t+1} - P_t + d_t - rP_t\} = 0 \qquad (4.27)$$

The conditional expectation of the term in braces, given information available at time t, must be zero. This implication can be tested by regressing the term in brackets against *any* available information at time t and rejecting the model if there are any significant explanatory variables. These regression or orthogonality tests rarely fail. Why do the volatility tests of precisely the same model almost universally indicate that the model is inadequate?

Shiller (1981b) argued that although both tests can be used to reject the model, the volatility tests have more statistical power. This means that there is a higher probability of rejecting the model using the volatility tests than the regression tests when the model is indeed not true. The reason for this is rather technical but, as Shiller argued, the volatility tests allow for price movements in the sample to be determined by information regarding dividends beyond the sample period. This argument suggests that if the volatility tests indicate rejection of the model when the regression tests do not, the verdict should be decided by the volatility tests.

There is, however, one problem with implementing the volatility tests. Before performing these tests, one must transform the data so that the resulting series has the property of stationarity. A stationary series cannot have a trend in either its mean or its variance. Sometimes it is difficult to determine if a particular series is stationary. For example, if dividend payments in successive years were $1, $2, $1, $2, $2, it would be difficult to judge whether the last dividend payment marked the beginning of a new trend.

It may well be the case that regression tests are more robust to deviations from stationarity than volatility tests are. In this case the verdict of the regression tests may be more accurate. Clearly, the econometrics of this issue deserve further consideration.

Assuming for the moment that the volatility tests are correct, what can account for the empirical results that indicate that the simple efficient markets model cannot explain the variance of stock prices? Shiller considered several alternatives. First, the stock market (and other financial markets) could be driven by fads or whimsy and the pricing equation has no relevance for the market. Two alternative hypotheses are less destructive to the enterprise of economic theory. One possibility is that the stock market is preoccupied with events of dramatic consequences but very low probabilities – for example, wholesale nationalization of U.S. industry or massive destruction through nuclear war. Because neither event occurred during the past century, actual dividend payments were not affected; yet the market could be reflecting changes in these low probability events. Shiller argued that this explanation could account for the excessive volatility of stock prices only if the probability of a major disaster changed substantially from period to period.

Another, less dramatic, explanation may be that the stock market equation may be misspecified. Interest rates or discount rates may not be constant from period to period but could exhibit considerable variation. If this were true, it means that the basic model of market equilibrium used in these tests is not correctly specified and this, rather than inefficiency, is the cause for the rejection of the tests.

Examining alternative models of market equilibrium should be a productive research strategy at this stage. There is sufficient ac-

cumulated evidence that simple models based on constant real interest
rates or constant risk premium are leading to rejections of the efficiency hypothesis. Researchers in various fields, from foreign
exchange to long-term bonds, are groping for new alternative models
of market equilibrium that are consistent with tests of market efficiency. One plausible model, considered in the next section, places
fluctuations in risk premia at center stage.

An alternative model of market equilibrium

Tests in bond, stock, and foreign exchange markets have
all been based on versions of Samuelson's martingale theorems for
efficient speculative markets. Samuelson's (1965) work allowed
for the presence of a risk premium, but in his model the risk premium
could not vary with the economic environment. LeRoy (1973) first
demonstrated that the strict martingale properties need not hold in
a model in which the risk premium varied endogenously in the
model. Lucas (1978a) developed these ideas further in a more general
model. These papers can provide a basis for alternative models of
market equilibrium that may not violate the tests of market efficiency.

The basic idea that motivates this work is that the appropriate
discount rate for security markets depends on the marginal value
of consumption today versus expected consumption in the future.
Securities are primarily held, after all, to transfer purchasing power
from one period to another, and thus the value to the payoff or
return to a security should depend on its value in increasing the
utility or the well-being derived from consumption. The marginal
utility or the contribution to well-being from additional consumption
will generally vary from period to period and this, in turn, means
that the discount rate will also vary.

To explore this idea further, consider a model in which an individual maximizes expected intertemporal utility from consumption
and can transfer purchasing power between periods by buying and
selling a risky security. Specifically, let the individual maximize

$$E \sum_{j=0}^{\infty} U(C_{t+j}) \tag{4.28}$$

subject to budget constraints of the form each period:

$$C_t \quad = \quad D_t X_{t-1} \quad + \quad P_t(X_{t-1} - X_t)$$

consumption = dividends received + net sales of the risky asset

where

C_t = consumption in period t

β = subjective discount factor ($\beta < 1$)

$U(\ )$ = utility from consumption $U' > 0$, $U'' < 0$

D_t = dividends paid in period t based on holdings of securities at $t - 1$

X_t = holdings of securities at time t that will result in dividend payments at time $t + 1$

P_t = price of the risky asset at time t measured in terms of the consumption good

At time t the individual knows the dividends that he receives and the current price of risky assets. The next period's price for risky assets, $\tilde{P}_{t+1}$, is random. An individual must decide on the amount of consumption today and thereby choose the quantity of risky assets to be carried forward into the next period.

A typical first-order condition for this maximization problem can readily be shown to be

$$U'(C_t)P_t = E\{\beta U'(C_{t+1})(D_{t+1} + P_{t+1})\} \qquad (4.29)$$

This has a nice intuitive interpretation. Holding an additional unit of the risky asset requires a sacrifice in terms of the marginal utility of the forgone consumption equal to $U'(C_t)P_t$, which is the left-hand side of the equation. On the margin, the loss in forgone consumption should be equated to the *expected* gain from holding an additional unit of the asset. The right-hand side measures the expected marginal gain in the utility from consumption, which can be gained by holding an additional unit of the risky asset. Holding an extra unit of the risky security entitles the consumer to the sum of the dividend and the market value of the security next period, weighted by the marginal utility of consumption the next period.

Grossman and Shiller (1981) show that this expression can be conveniently rewritten as

$$1 = E\{S_t(1 + r_t)\} \qquad (4.30)$$

where

$$S_t \quad = \frac{\beta U'(C_{t+1})}{U'(C_t)} = \quad \begin{array}{l}\text{marginal rate of substitution} \\ \text{of consumption between} \\ \text{periods } t \text{ and } t + 1\end{array}$$

$$1 + r_t = 1 + \frac{D_{t+1} + (P_{t+1} - P_t)}{P_t} = \quad \begin{array}{l}\text{one plus the} \\ \text{yield from} \\ \text{holding the} \\ \text{security}\end{array}$$

This equation states that the expected value of the product of the marginal rate of substitution in consumption and one plus the yield on the asset must be constant in every period.

To understand this expression, first consider the case in which S_t, the marginal rate of substitution of consumption, is a constant. It is easy to see that when S_t is constant, the discount rate is also constant. Using Equation (4.29), we find that the expected holding yield on securities is constant in all periods or

$$E\left\{ \frac{P_{t+1} - P_t}{P_t} + \frac{D_{t+1}}{P_t} \right\} = \text{ constant} \tag{4.31}$$

This is the familiar model of equilibrium returns that was rejected by the volatility tests.

In general, one might expect that the marginal rate of substitution would vary from period to period. To take an example, suppose that it was generally believed that tomorrow would bring "good times" and the level of consumption would be high. Because there is declining *marginal* utility of consumption, this means that the additional value of consumption tomorrow will be relatively low. In "good times" incremental consumption is worth less than in "bad times," and hence S_t will be lower than usual. This means, however, that yields on securities will be *higher* than average. To persuade an individual to defer consumption today and carry it forward to tomorrow when the incremental payoff will be worth less than usual, the required return on the asset must rise. More dramatically, as Shiller (1982) has pointed out, during the depths of the Great Depression, the expected yield on securities must have been high. After all, unless investors expected a substantial return on their investments, they would have wanted to sell their shares in an attempt to finance additional consumption during those bad times.

Conversely, if ''bad times'' are expected tomorrow, incremental consumption will be highly valued tomorrow. The required return on securities will, therefore, be lower than usual. Individuals have an increased demand for carrying assets into the future to ease the bad times and thus require a lower yield on the risky assets. Thus the expected profile of future consumption is crucial in determining the current equilibrium rate of return required in the market. As long as prospects of future consumption possibilities relative to current consumption possibilities vary over time, the equilibrium returns required in the market will vary.

This model has several important implications for evaluating tests of market efficiency. First, it is quite likely that different assets will have payoff structures that are related differently to future consumption prospects. Some assets will pay their highest returns in good times, whereas others will have their payoffs concentrated in bad times. It is evident that, holding other factors constant, assets that pay off handsomely in bad times will have lower required returns than other securities. This factor must be taken into account in assessing whether certain securities seem to be offering ''excess'' returns. Possibly these returns are not in excess at all but merely reflect the fact that certain securities have payoff structures that are very useful in increasing the utility derived from consumption.

In addition, this model suggests why tests of ''efficient markets'' based on models of a constant equilibrium expected return may be misleading. If expected marginal rates of substitution vary at all from period to period, equilibrium expected returns must also vary similarly. These movements in equilibrium expected returns could potentially account for the failure of some of the tests for efficient financial markets.

Grossman and Shiller (1981) attempt to account for the volatility of stock prices using this model. Choosing a utility function for each period of the form $U(C) = -\frac{1}{3}C^{-3}$ and using the actual historical series for consumption, they found that this model could, in principle, account for movements in stock prices from roughly 1890–1950. From 1950 to the present, however, stock market prices greatly exceeded the level of prices predicted by the theory. Thus even allowing for discount rates that vary with consumption, the stock market still remains somewhat of a mystery.

This, however, is one of the first attempts to implement this theory empirically. Because stock holdings are highly concentrated among the wealthy, perhaps aggregate consumption does not adequately reflect the change in consumption activities of this group. This is an interesting area for research because it links the behavior of financial markets with developments in the "real" economy and perhaps can account for some of the puzzling results of the volatility tests.

It is interesting to reflect on the intellectual motivation for much of this new research. A pattern quickly becomes evident. A theory of market efficiency is first formulated based on some very simple models of equilibrium returns. After some initial successful tests, more intensive and sophisticated empirical investigation reveals that the particular efficient markets model does not fit the data as precisely as was first thought. This, in turn, gives rise to new models of equilibrium returns and subsequent testing.

What is important is that the disconfirming evidence is used to argue against a particular model of equilibrium returns. It is not used, as it could be, to make blanket statements about the inefficiency of financial markets. Students of financial markets are reluctant to embrace Keynes's view that securities markets are sophisticated but irrational betting parlors. For better or worse, they have embraced efficient markets or rational expectations as a *research principle* or tool for deciding the validity of models of equilibrium price determination.

5

Empirical microeconomic models

Rational expectations is a concept that is useful for work in micro-economics as well as for macroeconomics and finance. This chapter will highlight some of the existing work in empirical microeconomic models by focusing on two areas in which expectations have long been recognized as important: agriculture and housing.

All the examples in Muth's (1960) paper were drawn from the area of agricultural economics. This was natural because, at that time, economic theory and econometrics had progressed quite far in this area. The work of Nerlove (1958) on adaptive expectations started an important econometric tradition in estimating agricultural supply relations that incorporated expectations.

Much of the interest in expectations and agricultural supply centered on the question of potential cycles or instabilities that was highlighted in the literature on the cobweb model, beginning with Ezekiel (1938). This model raised the possibility that when expectations of future prices were based on current prices, markets could be unstable.

Ezekiel assumed that production had to be planned one period in advance and that whatever output resulted was supplied inelastically to the market. Prices in any period, therefore, were demand determined, although actual harvests were based, in part, on what price the farmers anticipated.

The model consisted of a demand and supply relation:

$$Q_t^d = a - bP_t \qquad \text{demand} \tag{5.1}$$

$$Q_t^s = c + dP_{t-1} \qquad \text{supply} \tag{5.2}$$

The key feature in this simple linear model is that the supply decisions that are made in period $t - 1$ are based on the price prevailing at that time. Equating demand and supply in every period gives rise to a first-order linear difference equation that describes the evolution of prices over time:

$$P_t = \frac{a - c}{b} + \left(\frac{d}{-b} \right) P_{t-1} \tag{5.3}$$

Solving this equation for the path of prices over time yields

$$P_t = \left(\frac{a - c}{d + b} \right) + \left(\frac{-d}{b} \right)^t \tag{5.4}$$

The solution for the price consists of two terms. The first term is the long-run equilibrium price for the system. That is, in the absence of any disturbances, prices would be constant over time and, if this occurs, prices will settle down to $(a - c)/(d + b)$. If the system is perturbed, however, it will not immediately revert to the long-run equilibrium. The second term in the equation is a negative number raised to an integer that indexes the time period. As time evolves, the value of this term changes sign and the price will oscillate above and below its long-run equilibrium value. In fact, unless the stability condition, $|-d/b| < 1$ is satisfied, the oscillations will grow larger over time and the system will explode. The stability condition will be satisfied only if the slope of the supply curve exceeds the absolute value of the slope of the demand curve as drawn in traditional price-quantity space. Even if the stability condition is satisfied, damped oscillatory price and quantity movements will follow any disturbances to the system.

Figure 5.1 illustrates the operation of this phenomenon for a stable system. Assume that last year the system was at long-run equilibrium with price and quantity at P^*, Q^*. Planned production for the current year, accordingly, is also set for Q^*. Bad weather

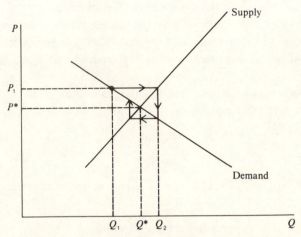

Figure 5.1 The cobweb model. The arrows indicate the path of prices resulting from an initial disturbance.

during the year, however, results in the actual harvest, Q_1, falling short of the planned harvest. Prices this year, P_1, are correspondingly higher than the long-run equilibrium for the system. Farmers will expect these high prices to persist, and hence planned harvests for the following year, Q_2, will exceed Q^*. Of course, this will lead to lower prices the following year, followed by low harvests, high prices, . . . and so on.

Farmers, trapped in this cycle, will feel most unfortunate. Just when they expect better than average prices, they find prices below average. And when they anticipate ''bad times,'' prices exceed their expectations. Farmers are not, however, victims of cruel fate; by not understanding the dynamics of the market they bring on the instability themselves.

Taking the model literally, we find that it would predict that most agricultural markets would be unstable. Demand for agricultural commodities is generally assumed to be quite inelastic, and hence the demand curve will be quite steep. Unless the aggregate supply curve is equally steep (an unlikely phenomenon), the model will be unstable. Casual observation suggests that instability in agricultural markets is not so pronounced as predicted by the theory.

Nerlove (1958) recognized that empirical work based on the simple cobweb model was likely to give misleading results. Borrowing from Cagan's (1956) work on hyperinflations, he introduced the concept of adaptive expectations to the modeling of agricultural markets.

Nerlove's version of the traditional agricultural model can be summarized in three equations:

$$Q_t^d = a - bP_t \qquad \text{demand} \qquad (5.5)$$

$$Q_t^s = c + dP_t^* \qquad \text{supply} \qquad (5.6)$$

$$P_t^* - P_{t-1}^* = \beta[P_{t-1} - P_{t-1}^*] \qquad \text{adaptive expectations}$$
$$0 < \beta < 1 \qquad (5.7)$$

where P_t^* is the expectation for prices at period t held in period $t - 1$.

There are two differences between the Nerlove and Ezekiel formulations. First, the supply curve is a function of the expected price that will not, in general, be equal to the last period's price. Second, price expectations are formed according to the adaptive expectations hypothesis, which states that the *change* in price expectations is equal to a fraction of the gap between the price that actually prevailed last period and the price that was anticipated for the last period. The adaptive expectations hypothesis can also be written as

$$P_t^* = \beta P_{t-1} + (1 - \beta)P_{t-1}^* \qquad (5.8)$$

which makes it clear that the price expected for period t is a weighted average of last year's price and the price expected for last year.

The rationale for this hypothesis was that farmers or any other economic actors have a notion of a "normal" price, P_t^*, which they adjust according to recent experience. If actual prices exceed what was anticipated, the normal price is adjusted upward; conversely, if actual prices fall short of what was anticipated, the expected price is adjusted downward. The coefficient "β," often known as the coefficient of adaptation, dictates how fast prices adjust to new information. If $\beta = 1$, the formula reduces to the Ezekiel model with $P_t^* = P_{t-1}$. However, the coefficient will generally fall short of unity and current information will only be partially utilized in adjusting expectations. As β approaches zero, the information about the latest price is increasingly ignored in formulating expectations.

The equations in Nerlove's model can be manipulated to yield a first-order difference equation in P_t, which, in turn, can be solved for the equilibrium path of prices:

$$P_t = \frac{a - c}{d + b} + \left\{ \left(\frac{-d}{b} - 1 \right) \beta + 1 \right\}^t \tag{5.9}$$

The solution for the time path of prices again consists of two terms. The first term is the long-run equilibrium for the system and is identical to the equilibrium in the cobweb system. The only difference between the models, therefore, rests in their respective dynamic properties. The second term in equation (5.9) dictates the dynamic response. The stability condition for this system is

$$\left| 1 + \beta \left(\frac{-d}{b} - 1 \right) \right| < 1 \tag{5.10}$$

which is more likely to be satisfied than the condition $|-d/b| < 1$, the stability condition for the cobweb model. The reason for this is that the parameter β acts as a brake on the system by making expectations somewhat sluggish to the arrival of new information. No matter what the slopes of the demand and supply curves are (as long as they have the correct sign), it is always possible to find a value of β that will create enough sluggishness in the system to ensure stability.

The stability condition for the Nerlove model reduces to the stability condition for the cobweb model when $\beta = 1$. For completeness it should be noted that, unlike the cobweb model, the adjustment to long-run equilibrium need not be oscillatory; it is possible if β is sufficiently low, to have a monotonic convergence to the equilibrium.

Because of the impact Nerlove's work had on popularizing the concept of adaptive expectations, it is important to stress, as he did, that an alternative formulation of the cobweb model could produce precisely the same dynamic behavior for prices and quantities as the adaptive expectations model did. In particular, let last period's price determine the *desired* supply but let the actual quantity supplied adjust slowly to the desired supply. Specifically,

$$\bar{q}_t^s = c - dP_{t-1} \qquad \text{desired supply} \qquad (5.11)$$

$$q_t^s - q_{t-1}^s = \alpha[\bar{q}^s - q_{t-1}^s] \quad \text{supply adjustment} \quad (5.12)$$

Combining these two equations with the preceding demand curve produces a model that is indistinguishable from the adaptive expectations model.

The rationale for this model is based on the distinction between long-run and short-run costs. The marginal cost of production will be higher in the short run than in the longer run when the firm is free to vary factors of production that are fixed in the short run. It is possible to combine this "partial adjustment model" with the adaptive expectation model to yield more complex dynamic specifications. The point, however, is that the "sluggishness" in supply response needed to stabilize the system need not stem from sluggishness of expectations.

Nerlove's formulation has had an immense impact on applied work in this area. As an indication of this, a recent survey by Askari and Cummings (1977) listed over five hundred studies on agricultural supply response in which variants of Nerlove's models were employed. From this large body of empirical evidence one might naively assume that the adaptive expectations hypothesis was clearly established over all other alternatives in this literature. The conclusion would not, however, be warranted. There have been only a few studies that even attempt to estimate an agricultural supply function that assumes rational expectations and still fewer that have tested for rational expectations.

Models of agricultural supply can be conveniently broken down into two groups: those in which storage of the commodity is possible and those for which it is not. The empirical evidence that exists pertains mostly to the latter group. The first section presents the theory of agricultural price and quantity determination when storage is not an option. The econometric issues are discussed and some empirical evidence is presented that provides support for the rational expectations hypothesis in a particular market.

The second section, "Models with storage," analyzes the more complicated case in which storage is possible and inventories of commodities are held for anticipated profit. The dynamics of price behavior are explored and contrasted to the case in which storage is not viable. The model is also employed to discuss the implications of futures trading. Several alternative theoretical approaches to this latter question are examined along with some empirical evidence.

The final section discusses an example of a microeconomic model of the housing market in which the rational expectations hypothesis may play a useful role. Although little empirical work has been done in this area, it indicates the scope for additional research by using rational expectations in empirical microeconomic models.

Models without storage

In a rational expectations model of agriculture supply the individual producer essentially asks the following question: "What price should I expect next year, taking into account the supply decisions of similarly situated producers so that my expectations for prices will, on average, be correct?" To answer this question, the individual producer must act as if he had a forecast of the demand curve facing the industry and knowledge of the cost curves for the industry.

Figure 5.2 illustrates the determination of the expected price in a rational expectations model with no storage. The demand curve in Figure 5.2 is drawn so that it reflects the expected values of the exogenous variables that determine the position of the curve. The supply curve depicts the quantity that producers would willingly supply at different values of expected prices. The expected price (and expected quantity) are determined by the intersection of the supply and demand curve at P^*.

To understand why P^* is the equilibrium expected price, suppose that producers expected the price to be a little higher, say P_1. At

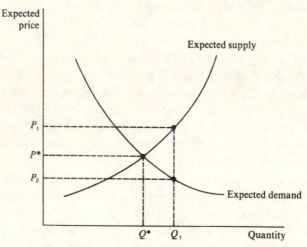

Figure 5.2 The determination of expected prices.

that price, production would be equal to Q_1, which, in turn, would lead to an average realized price below P_1. Producers would be overpredicting the actual price that would prevail. Similarly, if producers believed that the price was going to be less than P^*, their production decisions would lead to, on average, a higher price than anticipated. Only if prices were expected to be equal to P^* would expectations be fulfilled.

To analyze this model further, we consider a simple two-equation model:

$$Q_t^d = -bP_t + ey_t + \epsilon_t \qquad \text{demand} \qquad (5.13)$$

$$Q_t^s = c_{t-1}P_t^* + fW_t + \eta_t \qquad \text{supply} \qquad (5.14)$$

The demand curve in this formulation is totally conventional; quantity demanded is a decreasing function of the price and an increasing function of income (y_t) and is affected by a random disturbance (ϵ_t) that has mean zero and is serially uncorrelated. The supply curve is a function of the price anticipated in the previous period, a variable reflecting weather (W_t) and a mean zero, serially uncorrelated disturbance (η_t). Constant terms are suppressed for convenience.

The model is closed by assuming that in each period the price equilibrates the quantity demanded and the quantity supplied. In addition, expectations of prices are assumed to be formed rationally

$$_{t-1}P_t^* = E[P_t \mid I_{t-1}] \qquad \text{rational expectations} \qquad (5.15)$$

The equation for the expected price can be determined rather easily. First, equilibrium in the market requires that supply equals demand or

$$-bP_t + ey_t + \epsilon_t = c_{t-1}P_t^* + fW_t + \eta_t \qquad (5.16)$$

Taking the conditional expectation of both sides and rearranging yields the following expression for the expected price:

$$\frac{e_{t-1}\hat{y}_t - f_{t-1}\hat{W}_t}{c + b} = {}_{t-1}P_t^* \qquad (5.17)$$

where

$$_{t-1}\hat{y}_t = E(y_t \mid I_{t-1})$$

$$_{t-1}\hat{W}_t = E(W_t \mid I_{t-1})$$

The expected price, therefore, is a function of the expected values of the exogenous variables (income and weather) that drive the model.

Expected prices depend fundamentally on expectations of the variables that are determined outside the model at hand. Thus to determine expected prices in the market, producers act as if they both know the parameters of the model and have the forecasts for the exogenous variables. How are these forecasts to be determined?

One solution would be to build models that predict income and weather and, if necessary, further models to produce inputs for these models. Another alternative and the one used in the literature is to assume that the exogenous variables follow stable stochastic processes and use purely statistical techniques (time-series methods, for example) to obtain forecasts for the exogenous variables. Economic theory, therefore, is not generally employed to forecast the exogenous variables. Instead, these variables are forecasted by methods that a trained statistician would use depending only on the past history of the exogenous variables.

Two basic methods are available to obtain estimates of the parameters of the underlying model. The first approach is based on the principle of *instrumental variables* and essentially estimates the parameters of the supply and demand curves separately. The second method, based on *full-information* principles, estimates the supply and demand curve jointly.

The logic of the instrumental variables approach to rational expectations estimation depends on the idea that, under rational expectations, the expected price and the true price can only differ by unpredictable random error that is uncorrelated with any information available at time $t - 1$:

$$P_t = {}_{t-1}P_t^* + Z_t \tag{5.18}$$

$$E(Z_t \mid I_{t-1}) = 0$$

Substituting for the expected price in the supply equation yields

$$Q_t^s = cP_t + fW_t + (\eta_t - cZ_t) \tag{5.19}$$

The error term in this equation, $\eta_t - cZ_t$, is correlated with P_t requiring the use of some estimation technique besides ordinary least squares. As McCallum (1976) pointed out, instrumental variables techniques can be used in this case. Essentially, the price, P_t, is regressed on a set of variables that are uncorrelated with the composite error term. The regression equation is then used to calculate a forecast $\hat{P}_t$, which replaces P_t in equation (5.19). The equation then can be estimated by ordinary least squares to obtain consistent coefficient estimates. This approach has been developed further by Cumby et al. (1981).

The advantages of this approach are twofold: (1) It is fairly straightforward to use and requires only a selection of the "instruments" to be employed. (2) It allows an empirical investigator to focus solely, for example, on the supply equation without being concerned about the specification of the other equations in the model. This is particularly useful in a larger model in which there may be many other equations.

In some circumstances this latter "advantage" may actually be a disadvantage of the instrumental variables approach. More efficient estimates of parameters can often be obtained when information from all the equations can be utilized for the estimation of each equation. This general principle is especially relevant for rational expectations models because expectations are usually a property of the system as a whole. For example, in the agricultural model the expected price was a function of the parameters in both the supply and demand equations. Employing information about both the equations could improve the efficiency of the estimates.

By substituting the equation for the price expectation, equation (5.17), into the supply equation, we can now write the demand and supply system as

$$Q_t^d = -bP_t + ey_t + \epsilon_t \tag{5.13}$$

$$Q_t^s = \frac{ce}{c+b} {}_{t-1}\hat{y}_t - \frac{cf}{c+b} {}_{t-1}\hat{W}_t + fW_t + \eta_t \tag{5.20}$$

These two equations can be estimated jointly by maximum-likelihood methods leading to full-information estimates that embody the information from both equations. In this formulation the expected values of the exogenous variables ($_{t-1}\hat{y}_t$ and $_{t-1}\hat{W}_t$) are assumed to be known prior to the estimation. As Wallis (1980) indicates, it is also possible to estimate the stochastic processes for the exogenous variables jointly with the parameters of the model.

One important feature of the full-information approach should be noted. There are five variables contained in the equations (P_t, y_t, $_{t-1}\hat{y}_t$, $_{t-1}\hat{W}_t$, and W_t) but only four underlying coefficients (c, b, e, f) to be estimated. This indicates that there are overidentifying restrictions on the parameter estimates that can be used to test the model. By estimating the model with and without the constraints imposed, one can test whether the restrictions implied by the rational expectations hypothesis are valid. These tests must be, of course, joint tests of the rational expectations hypothesis and the maintained specification of the underlying model.

The rational expectations hypothesis does not have any implications for the type of stochastic process that commodity prices will follow. If movements in the demand curve or supply curve are serially correlated, then the price will, in general, also be serially correlated. The explicit equation for the price can be obtained by solving equations (5.13) and (5.20) for the price; it is evident that the stochastic processes of the exogenous variables in the model along with those of the disturbances to the supply and demand curves will determine the stochastic process for prices. In this model there is not even a presumption that prices need follow a random walk.

Empirical work on these models is quite limited as compared to the large number of studies employing the adaptive expectations hypothesis. One agricultural market that has been examined closely from the point of view of the rational expectations hypothesis is the broiler chicken industry. Without attaching any particular significance to this market, it has been a testing ground for the rational expectations hypothesis and thus deserves some scrutiny.

There are several reasons to believe that rational expectations may play a key role in characterizing supplier behavior in the broiler industry. First, the industry contains large-scale firms that have self-consciously adopted modern managerial techniques (e.g., linear programming models) to reduce costs. As an indication of the technical progress in this industry, between 1940 and 1972 the *nominal* price of broilers per pound fell three cents. This productivity increase can be attributed to both scientific developments and research to reduce feed costs. Second, industry leaders pay considerable attention to the price developments in related markets – this is prima facie evidence that they do not limit their information set to just past broiler prices.

Huntzinger (1979) estimated a rational expectations model of the broiler industry in what appears to be the first attempt to apply the rational expectations hypothesis to agricultural supply. He developed an instrumental variables technique that could be used for models with storage but found that, as industry spokesmen indicated, the storage option was not exercised for liveweight broilers. Using weekly data, Huntzinger estimated supply and demand relationships over the period and found that all the coefficients, including the one for the expected price, had the correct sign. In itself, this provides some indirect evidence for the rational expectations hypothesis. It is not difficult to construct examples in which instrumental variables estimation, applied to a model in which expectations were formed adaptively, would lead to the "wrong" sign on the expected price term.

Goodwin and Sheffrin (1982) took a full-information approach to this problem. Although their model differed in some minor respects (a different treatment of seasonality and the use of monthly rather than weekly data), they essentially employed the same basic framework as Huntzinger. They used seasonal, autoregressive, moving-average processes to forecast the exogenous variables and then estimated the full demand and supply system with full-information methods.

Goodwin and Sheffrin used their model to test the rational expectations hypothesis in three distinct ways. The first test was based on the overidentifying restrictions that are implied by the rational expectations hypothesis. The hypothesis of rational expectations could not be rejected by estimating the model in constrained and unconstrained forms.

A second test was based on the predictive efficiency of the rational expectations model. As Nelson (1975) first pointed out, as long as there is more than one underlying source of uncertainty in the model, a predictive equation based on a rational expectations model should have a lower forecast error variance than a predictive equation based on a time-series model for the price. The intuition for this result is that there is some information lost when different sources of uncertainty are aggregated into a single stochastic process. Goodwin and Sheffrin estimated their model and a time-series model over a subset of the data and then forecasted out of sample using both models. The price equation based on the rational expectations model outperformed the time-series model both within and beyond the sample period. Thus the model passed Nelson's predictive efficiency tests.

The final test was based on the orthogonality principle for conditional expectations. According to this principle, it should not be possible to improve the forecasts implied by the model with any information that was available at the time the forecast was made. To ensure that this test has sufficient statistical power (i.e., would lead to the rejection of the null hypothesis if it is false), one must select variables that are likely to contain additional information about the future behavior of prices. Fortunately, in this case there was a likely candidate for such a variable, namely, the price in the futures market for iced broilers. Although the empirical model determined the price for liveweight broilers, the futures market for this related commodity could provide useful information.

The actual price for broilers at time t was regressed on the price predicted by the rational expectations model and the price in the futures market (at the time the forecast was made) for a contract closing at time t. The coefficient on the futures price was not statistically significant, indicating that there was no additional information in the futures market. Thus in addition to passing the other two tests, the model passed the orthogonality test.

By bringing together the results of the three tests, one can make a strong case for the conclusion that in the broiler industry Muth's concept of rational expectations characterizes supplier behavior. The model passed the formal likelihood and prediction tests, and the information in a highly related futures market adds little, if any, predictive power. Although this, of course, is only a single market, it suggests that the recent contributions of Wallis and others to the econometrics of rational expectations can be applied to many agricultural markets.

Estimating rational expectation models forces the econometrician to specify carefully a number of important characteristics of the market. For example, the forecasting horizon and the time-series properties of the exogenous variables must be analyzed precisely in order to implement the estimation. This is a useful discipline, forcing explicit attention to many features of the market.

It is important to test the hypothesis of rational expectations in several ways. For agricultural models futures markets will be useful for these tests. Where futures markets are not available, the likelihood and predictive tests are still possible. Perhaps many of the over five hundred studies that used adaptive expectations would, in fact, be consistent with rational expectations.

Models with storage

Many agricultural commodities can be stored for at least some period of time. Introducing the possibility of storage enriches the model of the previous section in two ways. First, it introduces inventories of the commodities, and therefore equilibrium does not require that current production equal current consumption. Second, inventories can be held in anticipation of price increases, and thus, speculative motives are introduced into the model.

With storage, the basic agricultural model can be written as

$$Q_t^d = -bP_t \qquad \text{consumption demand} \qquad (5.21)$$

$$Q_t^s = c_{t-1}P_t^* + \eta_t \qquad \text{supply} \qquad (5.22)$$

$$I_t = \alpha(_tP_{t+1}^* - P_t) \qquad \text{inventory demand} \qquad (5.23)$$

$$Q_t^d + I_t = Q_t^s + I_{t-1} \qquad \text{equilibrium} \qquad (5.24)$$

$$_{t-1}P_t^* = E[P_t \mid I_{t-1}] \qquad \text{rational expectations} \qquad (5.25)$$

where I_t is the stock of inventories at the end of period t. In this formulation the exogenous variables in the supply and demand curves and the constant terms are suppressed and the error term is assumed to be serially uncorrelated.

The differences between the agricultural model with and without storage can be seen in equations (5.23) and (5.24). Equilibrium in the model requires that the total supply equal total demand. Total demand is composed of consumption demand and inventory demand, whereas total supply is equal to current production plus previously held inventories. This equilibrium condition can also be expressed in an alternative manner: The change in inventories equals the excess of current production over consumption demand.

Inventory demand is assumed to be a linear function of the anticipated price increase from period t to period $t + 1$. Muth (1961) derived this relationship by assuming that inventories are held by risk-averse expected utility maximizers. The paramer α, which measures the sensitivity of inventory demand to anticipated price change, is a function of the degree of risk aversion and the conditional variance of prices. The coefficient decreases as traders become less risk averse and also decreases as the conditional variance of prices decreases. It is also possible to derive an equation similar to equation (5.23) when speculators are risk neutral, but there are increasing marginal costs of carrying inventories.

Finding the equation for prices in this model is somewhat more difficult than in the model without storage. Substituting the consumption demand, inventory demand, and supply equations into the equilibrium condition yields an equation in the actual and expected values of prices of various periods and the disturbance:

$$\alpha_t P^*_{t+1} - (\alpha + b)P_t = (c + \alpha)_{t-1} P^*_t - \alpha P_{t-1} + \eta_t \quad (5.26)$$

One procedure for solving this equation involves first guessing the general form of the solution for the price equation, using it to calculate the appropriate expected values, substituting it into equation (5.26), and finally, calculating the implied restrictions on the coefficients. [An alternative solution procedure was used by Muth (1961).] This leads to the following equation for the price:

$$P_t = \lambda_1 P_{t-1} + \frac{1}{\alpha\lambda_1 - (\alpha + b)} \eta_t \quad (5.27)$$

where

$$\lambda_1 = 1 + \frac{1}{2} \frac{(b + c)}{\alpha} - \frac{1}{2} \frac{(b + c)}{\alpha} \sqrt{1 + \frac{4\alpha}{b + c}}$$

and $0 < \lambda_1 < 1$.

Technical details aside, the most interesting aspect of the equation for price is that prices will be correlated over time even when the disturbances (and the exogenous variables) exhibit no serial correlation. The reason for this is straightforward: Inventories smooth out the effects of supply disturbances. Unlike the case of a nonstorable commodity, a positive supply shock will affect current consumption and future consumption. Instead of letting the additional harvest go entirely into current consumption, inventory speculators will buy up some of the additional harvest and carry it into the future. Speculators are willing to do this because a good harvest makes prices temporarily low and profits can be gained by carrying stocks into the future and selling when prices are higher. This has the effect of generally dampening price fluctuations, thereby reducing the variance in prices. Disturbances in the current period will have a lingering effect into the future, which leads to correlations in price movements over time.

The model can shed light on Kendall's (1953) observation that weekly price movements in storable commodities seem to follow a random walk. As Muth (1961:327) noted, over short periods of time speculative inventory demands are more important in determining prices than are the flow supplies and demands. This statement can be interpreted in the current model as the hypothesis that the parameter α is large relative to the parameters b and c. This implies, using the equation for price, that the coefficient on lagged prices (λ_1) is close to 1, implying that prices resemble a random walk. The intuition behind this result is not difficult to understand. If speculators are very sensitive to price differentials, their activity will tend to eliminate predictable movements in prices. The result is that price changes will tend to be random over short periods or, in other words, prices will follow a stochastic process that appears close to being a random walk.

A number of authors have introduced futures markets into this model. As Peck (1976) noted, futures markets serve two roles. They facilitate storage by allowing, for example, grain storage activities to be separated from the price risk of holding inventories. They also, however, provide information that producers may be able to use in forecasting prices for their crops.

There have been several attempts to analyze futures markets in this basic agricultural model with storage. Peck considered a deterministic model with adaptive expectations and an arbitrary equation for futures prices. Turnovsky (1979) analyzed a stochastic model with rational expectations but assumed that, without futures markets, price expectations would be formed adaptively. Essentially, Turnovsky assumed that the introduction of futures markets would, in itself, convert a market with nonrational expectations to one with rational expectations. This attributes too much power to the introduction of futures markets. The introduction of a new market may certainly change information flows but should not drastically change the manner in which behavior operates.

In a provocative study, Cox (1976) analyzed the effects of the introduction of futures markets into an agricultural model in which agents had rational expectations. To model the effects of introducing futures markets, he used an idea contained in Muth's original article, namely, the last period's disturbance might be known only to a fraction of the participants in the market. With the introduction of futures markets this fraction was assumed to increase.

Cox first showed that with only a fraction of traders cognizant of the last period's disturbance, a regression of current prices on past prices would have a particular pattern. The coefficients on past prices should alternate in sign and decrease in absolute value as the lag length was increased. Increasing the fraction of informed traders leads to a decrease in the absolute value of all the coefficients on past prices and a smaller residual forecast error. When all traders were fully informed, only the coefficient on the last period's price should be significant; this was a consequence of the assumption that the error term in the model exhibited no serial correlation.

In his empirical work Cox considered a range of commodities, including onions, pork bellies, hogs, potatoes, cattle, and frozen concentrated orange juice. For each commodity he ran regressions of current prices on past prices for periods with and without futures markets. The market for onions was particularly interesting because futures trading was prohibited in that commodity in 1959 in the belief that it exacerbated price fluctuations in the spot commodity.

The results of the empirical analyses were generally supportive of the predictions of the theory. There were, however, a few anomalies. As an example, the unpredictability of onion prices (as measured by the coefficient of variation) decreased after futures trading was prohibited. This was the exception, however, rather than the rule.

Despite the generally favorable results, there are some potential pitfalls in interpreting his regression equations. Except for the case of onions, the period in which futures trading began naturally followed a period for which futures trading was absent. If other factors in the market changed with time, they could easily be confused with the impact of futures trading on the market. A related point is that the introduction of futures trading is certainly endogenous and thus the factors leading up to the introduction of a market may be confused with the effects of the market's introduction. Finally, only "successful" markets were considered in the analysis; there have been occasions in which experiments in futures trading began but the contracts were later withdrawn from the market.

Cox viewed the introduction of futures trading as the means by which a larger number of market participants could become informed of recent shocks to the market. There are several alternative ways to model the introduction of futures trading within the rational expectations framework. Muth suggested that the introduction of futures markets would alter the composition of those involved in speculative activities and lead to a different value for the parameter "α," which measured the sensitivity of inventory demand to anticipated price change. For example, if less risk-averse participants were attracted to the market, it is likely that inventory demand would be more responsive to changes in price. Differences in market risk aversion, therefore, is an alternative to differential information sets.

The volatility analysis, described in the previous chapter, may be relevant to an analysis of futures markets. It has long been argued by some that by bringing speculators into the futures market, spot prices for commodities become more volatile. Although Cox's results indicate little evidence directly supporting this position, the excessive "volatility" detected in stock and bond markets could possibly be present in futures markets and, in turn, affect the behavior of spot prices.

Finally, the microeconomic rational expectations work, also described in the previous chapter, can be brought to bear on this problem. This literature raised the possibility that the introduction of futures trading could reveal even privately held information to all market participants and could greatly expand the information utilized in the market.

It is clear that just postulating that market participants have rational expectations is only the first step to a complete analysis of the market. A full analysis involves specifying, at the minimum, risk preferences and information sets. Rational expectations provide a useful departure point for analyzing the implications of various alternative assumptions; it is the beginning not the end.

Housing investment and price appreciation

It is commonly believed that the rapid rise in real housing prices throughout much of the United States during the 1970s could be attributed to speculative activity on the part of the public. Belief in continued inflation, it has been argued, increased the demand for housing as a store of value and continually pushed up its price. As housing speculation became feverish, some observers attributed the behavior of prices to irrational behavior. However, it is not difficult to sketch a theory of rational price speculation based on a microeconomic model of the housing market.

This model of the housing market builds on two different themes: the interaction of taxes and inflation and the role of capital gains in the theory of investment. First, the interaction of inflation and taxes is particularly important for owner-occupied housing. Individuals who own their own home are permitted to deduct interest payments and property taxes from their income taxes, but the imputed rental income from living in the homes is not included in taxable income. Moreover, capital gains taxes upon the sale of a home can generally be avoided by either buying another home or taking advantage of certain exclusions available in the law. As deLeeuw and Ozanne (1981) and others have argued, these provisions confer a tax advantage on owner-occupied homes relative to other investments. If nominal interest rates rise roughly point for point with inflation, then inflation actually reduces the effective cost of housing. Homeowners can deduct the higher nominal interest payments from their income taxes but will generally not pay any additional taxes on the higher nominal value of their home. Thus inflation increases the attractiveness of owner-occupied housing.

Anticipated capital gains on housing, like any other asset, should influence its demand. Abel (1980) has analyzed the role of capital gains on investment in an intertemporal model of capital accumulation based on the theory of the firm. For housing investment it is useful to separate the demand for housing by consumers from the decisions of competitive firms producing housing. This approach, based on the work of Witte (1963), has been taken by a number of writers, including Kearl (1979) and Poterba (1980) who integrated the housing taxation issues with the investment dynamics. The housing model to be presented subsequently, due to Poterba, has the same mathematical structure as the Blanchard (1981) model discussed in Chapter 3, so that only a brief theoretical treatment is required.

To analyze the demand side of the market, one should think in terms of the fiction that there is actually a rental market for owner-occupied housing. The yearly "rentals" in this market would equal the carrying cost of buying a house for a year and then selling it at the end of the year. The costs of doing this would depend on the price of housing, Q; the depreciation rate, δ; the income tax rate, t; the interest rate, i; the property tax rate, u; the general inflation rate, π; and the rate of real price appreciation for housing, $\dot{Q}/Q$. The formula for the rental cost of housing in this case is

$$\text{rental cost} = Q\left[\delta + (1 - t)(i + u) - \pi - \frac{\dot{Q}}{Q}\right] \quad (5.28)$$

The intuition behind this formula is straightforward. The price of the house, Q, represents the initial outlay that an investor must make to acquire the asset. During the year the asset depreciates at the rate δ and the investor must pay interest and property taxes on his investment. This accounts for the first two terms in the brackets. The cost of renting the house, however, is decreased by any nominal price appreciation of the asset that is accounted for by the last two terms in the brackets. In short, the rental cost per dollar of investment is composed of depreciation, interest and taxes, less any price appreciation.

The rental cost formula takes into account the special tax treatment of housing. Interest and property tax payments $(i + u)$ are tax deductible but neither the rental or the total capital gain on housing $[\pi + (\dot{Q}/Q)]$ is taxed. As the formula indicates, as long as nominal interest rates increase point for point with inflation, the rental cost of housing will decline with inflation because the inflation premium in interest rates is deductible from personal income taxes. If interest payments were not deductible, the higher nominal interest rates would just balance the faster appreciation rate of the house, leaving the rental price unchanged. Tax deductibility, however, means the government pays part of the higher interest rates and the rental cost, therefore, falls.

The rental demand price for a unit of housing, $R(H)$, is a decreasing function of the existing stock of housing, H. In each period it is assumed that the rental demand price for a unit of housing adjusts to equal the rental cost of providing an additional unit:

$$R(H) = Q\left[\delta + (1 - t)(i + u) - \pi - \frac{\dot{Q}}{Q}\right] \quad (5.29)$$

This expression can be rewritten as a differential equation in the price of housing:

$$\dot{Q} = -R(H) + zQ \quad (5.30)$$

where

$$z = \delta + (1 - t)(i + u) - \pi$$

The assumption of perfect foresight has been built into the analysis by assuming that the actual change in real housing prices is equal to what was anticipated. This will play an important part in the dynamics of the model.

The production side of the model is straightforward. The change in the stock of housing $(\dot{H})$ equals the excess of new production (NH) over depreciation (δH):

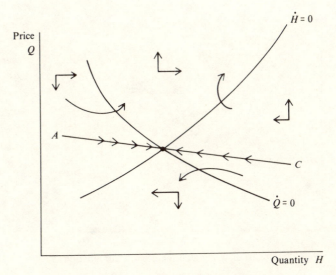

Figure 5.3 Phase diagram for the housing model.

$$\dot{H} = NH(Q) - \delta H \qquad (NH' > 0) \qquad (5.31)$$

New housing production is an increasing function of the real price of housing as additional resources are drawn into the production of housing as the price increases.

The phase diagram for the two-equation system consisting of equations (5.30) and (5.31) is depicted in Figure 5.3. The $\dot{Q} = 0$ locus is the set of pairs of prices and stocks of housing for which the market is in equilibrium and there are no anticipated capital gains or losses. It is equivalent to the demand curve for housing when there are no anticipated capital gains. Above the locus, housing prices are increasing, because at higher prices the rental cost of housing is increased. To maintain equilibrium in the rental market, there must be anticipated capital gains on housing that lower the rental cost so that it continues to equal the existing rental demand price of housing.

The $\dot{H} = 0$ locus is the set of pairs of prices and housing stocks along which the stock of housing remains constant. The locus is

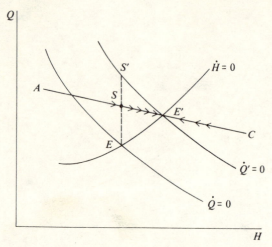

Figure 5.4 An unanticipated increase in the inflation rate.

upward sloping because at higher stocks of housing, depreciation is higher, and therefore a higher price for housing is needed to bring forth enough production to equal the higher depreciation. Above the locus, prices induce a production level that exceeds depreciation and the housing stock increases.

The phase diagram exhibits saddle-point instability with the stable arm, AC, being downward sloping. The reason for this instability rests essentially with the assumption of perfect foresight of capital gains and losses, which implies that high housing prices necessitate rising prices to equilibrate the rental market, whereas low prices necessitate falling prices. This dependence of the rate of change of prices on the level of prices in this way is what causes the saddle-point instability. As in the discussion of the Blanchard (1981) model in Chapter 3, it is necessary to assume that the economy is always located somewhere on the stable arm to ensure convergence to long-run equilibrium.

The dynamics of the model can be illustrated with a simple experiment. Assume that in Figure 5.4 the economy is in equilibrium at point E. Then, it is announced that the inflation rate has jumped suddenly to a higher level, which will be maintained permanently.

The higher inflation, which is a favorable development to the housing market, shifts the $\dot{Q} = 0$ to $\dot{Q}' = 0$.

The price of housing immediately jumps to the point S on the stable arm at the existing stock of housing. Prices then decrease and the housing stock increases on the path to the new equilibrium E'. Market participants know that housing prices will be falling on the path toward equilibrium as new production increases the stock of housing. Because they expect these capital losses, the price does not jump immediately to S', which would be the short-run equilibrium if the market ignored the future capital losses during the transition to the new equilibrium. In this case the assumption of perfect foresight limits fluctuations in the price of housing as compared to a model in which expectations were myopic.

Poterba (1980) developed a discrete-time version of this model and calibrated it by employing empirical elasticity estimates derived from other studies of the housing market. Using the empirical model, he simulated the effects of both permanent and temporary inflation shocks as well as shocks that were anticipated. Because the model was simply calibrated with existing estimates and neither estimated directly nor tested, its predictions can only be suggestive. Nonetheless, it was striking that even temporary inflation shocks had important effects on the housing market.

It would be instructive to conduct a detailed empirical investigation by comparing the predictions of alternative models of expectations formation to the actual dynamics of housing prices and housing stocks. It may be that other expectation mechanisms were governing the housing market in the 1970s. Rational expectations could, in principle, account for the dynamics of an apparent ''speculative boom'' and it could be interesting for policy purposes to know if that indeed was the case. It should, however, be pointed out that the ''speculation'' in this model is not a phenomenon that is distinct from the demand for housing. With rational actors any anticipated price changes on assets become an integral part of the supply and demand picture.

Many other microeconomic models need reconsideration from the rational expectations point of view. For example, a modified cobweb model has been used by Freeman (1971) to study the market for engineers and scientific personnel. This model, of course, predicts an eventual glut of personnel following an initial boom. A rational expectations model would predict that gluts would occur only if individuals incorrectly forecasted the persistence of the factors causing the boom. Policy implications stemming from the two approaches are quite different. If the modified cobweb model is true, the U.S. Labor Department can make plans well in advance to deal with the inevitable glut of specialized scientific personnel. In a rational expectations model of the labor market, forecasts of future business and government demands for output would be in order.

6

Rational expectations in practice

Most political observers are accustomed to optimistic economic forecasts from the executive branch of the U.S. government. They were not, however, quite prepared for the first forecasts or "scenarios" concocted by economists associated with the Reagan Administration. These forecasts suggested that inflation would fall from the double-digit levels prevailing during 1981 to 6.5 percent by 1982 and to 4.5 percent by 1983. This dramatic reduction in inflation was not intended to be the consequence of a massive recession. On the contrary, real output was predicted to grow rapidly at the same time that inflation was falling.

This feat was to be accomplished by Reagan's proposed economic plan, consisting of personal and corporate tax cuts, regulatory reform, and a sustained reduction in the rate of money growth. Existing econometric models did not predict so rosy an economic scenario from this plan as did Administration forecasts. The combination of "easy" fiscal policy and "tight" money was viewed by some forecasters to be, on net, stimulative and to lead to an increase rather than a decrease in the inflation rate. Other forecasters foresaw a collision between these monetary and fiscal policies leading to high interest rates and diminished growth. The personal tax rate cuts based on the Kemp–Roth formula of 10 percent cuts in marginal rates for three years were particularly disturbing, as they appeared to boost consumption at the expense of investment spending and

177

thus diminish capital formation. Why did the Administration forecasts differ so sharply from those of the more conventional forecasters?

As *Washington Post* columnist Hobart Rowen (1981) wrote, the answer was "nothing more or less than the old theory of 'rational expectations.' " The Office of Management and Budget had contracted with John Rutledge of the Claremont Economic Institute to use a model that he had developed to provide forecasts for the Reagan Administration. Rutledge's model was based on some of the ideas discussed in the rational expectations literature. In particular, the combination of easy fiscal and tight money policies would not be inflationary. A tight money policy would immediately lower the private sector's estimates of future inflation rates so that a painless disinflation policy was possible. The supply-side tax cuts would spur savings, investment, and growth without fueling inflation. Inflation was largely determined by inflationary expectations that could be directly altered by a committed posture of monetary restraint. Despite its larger structure, the Claremont model worked essentially the same way as the simplest rational expectations models in which an anticipated decrease in money growth rates would lead simply to lower inflation rates and would not precipitate a recession.

As Rutledge stated in an interview with Rowen (1981), "Our view of the world is that it is expectation-driven. The only value the past has is in teaching people to think about the future. What you need to do is to provide them with signals that they view as reliable, and they will organize their lives around those signals." If the government provided the correct signals about the future course of monetary policy, a reduction in inflation rates could be readily achieved.

This simple version of a rational expectations model was to play an important political role in selling the Reagan economic plan. The Republicans had campaigned on a platform calling for substantial personal and business tax cuts. They also promised that their policies would reduce inflation and spur economic growth. Conventional macroeconomic models suggested that higher growth meant higher inflation and lower inflation could only be achieved with slower economic growth. Simple rational expectations models promised an answer to this conundrum – inflation could be reduced without sacrificing real growth by a policy of announced reductions in the money growth rate. Thus simple rational expectations models could make the economic proposals contained in the Republican economic platform appear to work.

The press and most of the private sector were not convinced by the new economic scenario. Predictably, the creators, owners, and staff of the existing econometric models thought that the ideas on which the forecasts were based were simply untested speculations. The Claremont model had no official track record and had not been subject to any academic scrutiny. The press echoed these views and generally expressed skepticism over the forecasts.

These forecasts also failed to receive any support from the influential founders of rational expectations theory. *Business Week* (1981:14) revealed that Robert Lucas thought little of this effort. As they reported: ''Lucas says he is 'pessimistic' that the rational expectations theory can ever be used to develop mathematically quantifiable forecasts and that short-term forecasts, at any rate, are essentially extrapolations of current conditions. 'And for that purpose,' he says, 'rational expectations doesn't have much to add.' ''

This episode ended with the Reagan Administration backing down somewhat from their original forecasts. Council of Economic Advisors' Chairman Murray Weidenbaum engineered a compromise within the Administration to change the forecasts used in the budget. The forecast for inflation was increased to 7.7 percent (from 6.5) in 1982 and to 6.6 (from 4.5) in 1983. A very deep recession later ensued, which brought the inflation rate down by traditional means.

One unfortunate aspect of this affair was that the press associated rational expectations with the more extreme flexible price models in which anticipated money growth solely affected prices. It left the impression that rational expectations was a theory shared only by a monetarist fringe and not an idea that had profoundly influenced thinking in both macroeconomic and microeconomic theory. In short, the rational expectations hypothesis got a bad press.

The episode did demonstrate, however, that few economists were persuaded by the evidence accumulated during recent years in support of the extreme versions of the rational expectations macro model. It was hard to find economists supporting, even in principle, the rational expectations-related ideas of the Reagan Administration. Although it could work, in principle, the evidence was lacking. As Thomas Sargent (1981b:2) stated, "Economists do not now possess reliable, empirically tried and true models that can enable us to predict precisely how rapidly and with what disruption in terms of lost output and employment such a regime change will work its effects."

Sargent (1981b) recognized that the case for an immediate turn around in the inflation rate following a change in policy regimes would have to rest on additional evidence. In his view, several hyperinflations during the 1920s (Austria, Hungary, Poland, and Germany) provided unique laboratory experiments for the study of regime change. One of the most striking features in all these cases was the dramatic and sudden stabilization of the price level and the exchange rate that followed drastic monetary and fiscal reform. These hyperinflation episodes did not end gradually but stopped abruptly and the apparent momentum to the inflationary process simply disappeared. Was this a lesson for disinflation in the 1980s?

Critics argued that this evidence was not relevant for reducing inflation in less dramatic situations. During hyperinflations, monetary denominated long-term contracts virtually disappear as no one wishes to enter into commitments whose value changes capriciously from day to day. Without long-term contracts and related nominal commitments, the frictions that make it difficult to engineer a painless disinflation policy also disappear. Because business dealings are constantly in the process of renegotiation, a currency reform need not disrupt the flow of commerce. If inflation became so severe that it effectively abrogated existing long-term nominal contracts, then regime changes need not disrupt economic activity. Until that time, however, costs of a rapid disinflation could be quite significant.

Lucas (1980b) anticipated the Reagan Administration's early flirtation with rational expectations in an article concerning the proper role for economic policy. The legacy of stagflation and poor record of economic growth in the 1970s weakened public confidence in traditional demand management policies. A symptom of this change, Lucas (1980b:204) noted, was ''Arthur Laffer's influential 'Laffer curve' and Arthur Okun's proposal for controlling inflation by a complex system of taxes and subsidies on individual producers . . . both can be supported by theory of sorts, provided one uses the term 'theory' with sufficient looseness.'' These ideas flourished in the atmosphere of disillusionment with macroeconomic policy. To this list of popular, untested ''theories'' we can now add the simplest rational expectation models of the early Reagan Administration.

Lucas attributed the public's disillusionment to prior expectations that demand management policy was well founded and well understood.

> The stagflation error did not occur in the privacy of the seminar room, a puzzle of interest to professionals only. It occurred *after* the idea of a stable inflation–unemployment trade-off had become accepted by the public generally as *the* central construct in discussing macroeconomic policy, and *after* wide public acceptance of the ideas that movements along the Phillips curve were technically within the control of economic managers. (1980b:203–4)

The embarrassment was public.

Explaining the atmosphere of disillusionment within the profession is a more difficult task. It is certainly possible to account for the events of the 1970s with a modern Keynesian macro model that incorporates the natural rate hypothesis along with adaptive expectations. To do so requires special attention to wage and price controls, disappearance of anchovies, grain shortages, OPEC shocks, as well as to policy actions. Alan Blinder's (1979) *Economic Policy and the Great Stagflation* is an interesting effort along these lines. Specific failures of macroeconomic policy cannot be the sole cause of professional agnosticism on many key macro issues.

The development of rational expectations theory itself is largely responsible for the atmosphere of professional disillusionment. Lucas's (1976) critique of existing econometric models, discussed in

Chapter 3, was especially important. His critique was neither model nor theory specific and applied universally across all existing macro models. The critique had the effect of changing the way the profession viewed the econometric models. It was not simply that these models would on occasion produce large forecast errors – this defect seemed amenable to improvement. Instead, Lucas convinced the profession that the econometric models were essentially elaborate codifications of existing decision rules. They might well be efficient autoregressive machines that are useful for tracking short-term business cycle developments; but they were not suitable for policy evaluation purposes when the proposed policy was likely to change the actual operating characteristics of the system. As the profession began to view the models differently (a true shift in vision), the existing econometric models were lost as a hard-earned tool. Simulations with the models were no longer persuasive and no new tools, free of the critique, were apparent on the horizon.

Aside from adding to the atmosphere of disillusionment, what did the work in rational expectations add to our perspectives on the economy? There were both direct and indirect developments stemming from this new work. The direct developments centered around new models of the business cycle and the theoretical and empirical work that focused on the short-term efficacy of monetary policy. Indirectly, rational expectations altered the program of research, affecting both the substantive content and style of subsequent research.

Standing at the center of the theoretical developments in macroeconomics during the 1970s was Lucas's model of the business cycle theory discussed in Chapter 2. The reconstruction of business cycle theory within an equilibrium model was based on two different strands of thought. First, there was substantial opportunity for individuals to alter their labor supply to take advantage of temporary, perceived fluctuations in their compensation. Labor supply decisions were fundamentally grounded in an intertemporal framework, and consequently, labor supply could vary sharply over the business cycle to take advantage of perceived opportunities. Second, economy-wide information was not a free good, and individuals were limited in the information that was available to them. A combination of

these two elements – intertemporal substitution and limited information – allowed unpredictable monetary shocks to cause fluctuations
in labor supply, output, and employment.

Although the ingenuity of Lucas's arguments has been appreciated,
there is some dissatisfaction with the two basic strands to his model.
The direct evidence on intertemporal substitution is not strong enough
to dispel the doubts of skeptics who questioned whether labor supply
decisions were truly that sensitive to intertemporal variations in
compensation. One of the few empirical studies to find support for
intertemporal substitution over the business cycle was the early
work by Lucas and Rapping (1970). They, however, assumed that
agents formed expectations adaptively; when Altonji (1981) reex-
amined their work by using the hypothesis of rational expectations,
the evidence disappeared.

Of more concern is the information assumptions. With the steady
parade of information available in the daily papers and the heightened
awareness of economic phenomena, it may seem peculiar to base
theories on a paucity of information. As Hall (1980:23) noted, ''a
large amount of information about prices, wages, employment,
unemployment, and other aggregate variables is available virtually
instantaneously and essentially for free. It is hard to see how the
hypothesis of the theory of monetary non-neutrality on account of
limited information can apply when such a wealth of information
is available.'' Both the doubts over the intertemporal substitution
mechanism and the information assumptions have persisted, leaving
many economists unconvinced by Lucas's reconstruction of business
cycle theory. Lucas (1980a:713) recognized the point in a survey
article: ''I have tried to avoid claiming too much for the particular
examples of equilibrium models that now exist. There is no point
in letting tentative and, I hope, promising first steps harden into
positions that must be defended at all cost.'' Future equilibrium
models of business cycles may look different from Lucas's prototype.
Lucas did, however, demonstrate that equilibrium models could
account for most of the stylized features of business cycles.

Propositions about the short-run ineffectiveness of monetary policy
have met the same fate as Lucas's model, that is, initial excitement
followed by a more sober assessment of their limitations. As indicated

in Chapter 2, the invariance or ineffectiveness propositions depended on the dual assumptions of the neutrality of money and a wage–price process that essentially replicates a Walrasian system. In the face of some obvious nonneutralities, McCallum (1980) suggested that the ineffectiveness proposition should be recast to state that the parameters of the money supply process could not affect the deviation of output from capacity (or full employment) output. This would allow, for example, for anticipated changes in the money growth rate to affect the capital stock (and thus capacity) through changes in real interest rates but not affect the gap between output and capacity.

Even this reconstruction of the invariance proposition proved not to be robust to small changes in model specifications. When market participants have access to current information such as interest rates, the systematic part of the money supply process may, in some cases, influence the probability distribution of the gap between output and capacity. Moreover, it is now common knowledge that certain forms of "rational" wage contracts will also permit the monetary authorities to have some leverage over real variables. These theoretical findings have led McCallum (1980:738), who is highly sympathetic to rational expectations, to conclude that "it seems difficult to sustain the position that the policy ineffectiveness proposition is applicable to the U.S. economy."

The empirical work on the ineffectiveness proposition followed a similar story. Barro's (1977a, 1978) early work suggested that the economy could possibly be described by the simple aggregate supply relations for which systematic monetary policy had no effect on output. However, the empirical findings were clouded by subtle identification problems that raised questions about the interpretations of the empirical equations. In addition, the more recent empirical work that tested separately for rationality and neutrality has turned up evidence against neutrality. Finally, the simple aggregate supply relationships did not fare well against models that featured price inertia.

Thus the most direct and immediate contributions to macroeconomics from the work on rational expectations are still controversial.

But the rational expectations paradigm has had profound effects on the general development of macroeconomics and this, perhaps, is its most significant contribution.

The growing acceptance of rational expectation ideas removed an "expectational crutch" that existing macroeconomic models relied on. It soon became apparent that the dynamics of the models (e.g., the MPS model) depended rather intimately on arbitrary and ad hoc models of expectation formation. In particular, the slow adjustments to long-run equilibrium following exogenous shocks could often be explained by the slow adjustment of inflation expectations. As the concept of rational expectations became popular, these arbitrary adjustment mechanisms for expectations were no longer satisfactory. Without them, however, the models would no longer retain the Keynesian features that were deemed essential. This discovery forced economists who believed that the economy did have important Keynesian features to search for alternative means to achieve their desired results.

The result was the birth of a new institutionalism. This was not a continuation of the institutionalism of Ayers, Commons, and Veblen but a theoretically inspired movement to explain institutions, such as labor contracts, in terms of individual-maximizing behavior. One important example of this phenomenon was the study of the explicit and implicit agreements between firms and workers that were based on motives such as risk sharing, moral hazard, and efficient response to new information. This literature looks beyond the surface details of agreements to show that the existence of contracts can be explained by the overall stochastic pattern of key economic variables rather than just their realizations or in Nordhaus's (1976:623) term "the economic climate rather than the economic weather." Even critics of many aspects of the rational expectations approach, such as Solow (1980), call for renewed efforts in modeling firm–worker behavior.

A second aspect of this new institutionalism is renewed interest in the framework of monetary policy. The simplest rational expectations models revealed the important role that money supply "rules" have on the dynamic behavior for output and prices. These money supply rules are, however, the outcome of a complex political process. These outcomes are influenced by the structure of institutions governing the conduct of policy and could be changed if the institutional environment were altered. The renewed academic interest in gold and other commodity standards is an aspect of this rediscovery of institutions.

Perhaps more important than the new institutionalism is the project that Lucas outlined for the future course of macroeconomics. By demonstrating that it was possible to construct general equilibrium macro models based on individual optimizing behavior that capture the stylized features of business cycles, Lucas set new standards for business cycle theory and macroeconomic model building. A new set of mathematical tools was developed to analyze stochastic macro models. As Lucas (1980a) has emphasized, the questions that can be addressed are limited by the tools that are available. By expanding the scope of discourse, it enables the profession to address new sets of problems. In particular, the tools developed for stochastic models are useful for analyzing the operating characteristics of economic systems under alternative policy rules – an important alternative to analyzing the effects of one-time interventions.

These achievements are likely to persist. Even James Tobin who has for many years fought against simple versions of what he termed "monetarism" believes that this work will have lasting influence. Putting what he called the second monetarist counterrevolution into perspective, Tobin noted,

> The ideas of the second counter-revolution are too distinctive and too powerful to be lost in the shuffle. They are bound to shape whatever orthodoxy emerges. The durable ideas are more methodological than substantive – internally consistent derivations of rational expectations and rational behavior, embodied in the structural equations of a general equilibrium macroeconomic model. These ideas are already being mobilized not just to exalt the Invisible Hand but to explain the causes and effects of informational

imperfections, long-term contracts and other
commitments, incompleteness of capital markets,
liquidity constraints, and many other phenomena of
common observation. As the process bears fruit,
Keynesian problems will be interpreted in a new light
but will not disappear or be dismissed as theoretical
impossibilities. There will be plenty of room for
compensatory demand management, both in theoretical
models and in real economies, and improved
understanding how to use it. (1980:41–2)

Although all economists involved in this work would not agree with
Tobin on its eventual outcome, they could share in the spirit of
inquiry within this new framework.

This approach has already produced new and provocative theories
and insights that were unlikely to have emerged without the focus
on intertemporal, stochastic macroeconomic models. Important examples of this research include the recent work by Kydland and
Prescott (1980) and Barro (1980b) on fiscal policy.

Kydland and Prescott developed a simple model of business cycles
based on microeconomic models of utility maximization and investment decisions. By allowing for lags in installing capital, they
showed that stochastic, equilibrium models of this type could produce
dynamic patterns for output that resemble actual business cycle
patterns. They introduced a public sector into their model that provided a public good that must be financed by either debt or taxes.
By introducing this rudimentary model of the public sector, they
analyzed whether tax rates should be varied over the course of the
business cycle in order to stabilize output.

Kydland and Prescott concluded that tax rates should *not* be varied
to stabilize output. To understand their reasoning, one should first
note that tax changes in their model could stabilize output by affecting
the relative prices of work and leisure over time. Stabilizing output
would require making leisure expensive (i.e., relatively low taxes
on labor supply) when output is low and making leisure cheap
(relatively high tax rates on labor supply) when output is high. It
is because individuals in this model view labor supply in neighboring

periods as close substitutes that changes in the relative price of leisure over time can affect labor supply and thereby stabilize output.

It is precisely *because* labor supply is highly substitutable over time that tax rates should not vary with the business cycle. This conclusion follows almost directly from the literature on optimal taxation, which originated with Ramsey (1927). One important lesson from this literature is that goods that are highly substitutable should have similar rates of tax. Otherwise, the consumption patterns induced by the differential tax rates can sharply reduce welfare. In this example labor supply in neighboring periods are close substitutes and should, therefore, have similar tax rates. Varying tax rates over the business cycle, or in response to temporary changes in government expenditure, will cause welfare losses as closely substitutable goods will have different rates of tax.

This strong and rather striking conclusion follows closely from the structure of their model. As Feldstein (1980) pointed out, the result hinges on the assumption that changes in labor supply during a business cycle reflects intertemporal substitution of leisure by workers. If fluctuations in employment arise for Keynesian reasons (changes in the effective demand for labor), then tax rate changes that stabilized output could possibly improve welfare. Nonetheless, Kydland and Prescott's (1980) work is important in two respects. First, it illustrated and developed techniques for analyzing fiscal policy in equilibrium models. In addition, it pointed out the potential welfare distortions that could be induced by varying tax rates (such as the investment credit) over the business cycle.

Barro (1980b) arrived at the similar conclusion that tax rates should not vary to finance temporary government expenditure through a different route. He began with the view that, as a first approximation, individuals fully discount the future taxes necessary to service the public debt and thus tax and debt finance have similar macroeconomic effects. What then determines the actual mix of tax and debt finance? Barro argued that the government sets tax rates to minimize the deadweight burden from collecting taxes. He developed a model in which the tax collection technology was such that this deadweight loss was minimized when expected tax rates were constant over time.

Barro's models had several testable implications. Temporary changes in government expenditure (such as wars) should induce positive movements in debt issue. In addition, debt issue should be countercyclical as the government minimizes collection costs by not changing tax rates for temporary movements in income. Thus as income and tax collections fall, deficits increase. Barro tested these and several other implications of this theory over the course of this century since World War I. Although not all the implications of his theory were precisely borne out by the data, it remains a suggestive study and an alternative to the view that actual tax and debt policy can be explained as an attempt to stabilize the economy.

Even for those economists uncomfortable with many of the assumptions of the equilibrium macro models, the rational expectations approach has had a profound effect on the use and interpretation of the models. Any list of the major developments would have to include:

1. The necessity for distinguishing between the effects of anticipated and unanticipated policy actions. This is important regardless of whether the models are neutral with respect to anticipated policy changes.
2. The recognition that the optimal control problem is intrinsically more subtle and complicated when economic actors are rational. This general topic includes the problem of the inconsistency of optimal plans and the need to specify policy rules in order to calculate the response of the private sector to changing economic conditions.
3. The development of new econometric and simulation techniques to analyze models in which expectations are formed rationally. In particular, models in which expectations of future variables affect current prices require methods of analysis that were just recently developed. Again, this is just as important for models sharing many traditional Keynesian features as Blanchard's (1980) simulation study indicates.
4. The careful examination of all estimated equations to see if they would be likely to change when the policy environment or the stochastic processes of economic variables changes, according to Lucas's critique of econometric models. Equations that had previously been thought to be structural equations (e.g., consumption functions) now are seen to have "structures" that are not invariant to changes in the economic environment.

These developments have for the most part been technical in the precise sense of changing the *techniques* acceptable for economic analysis. It is a challenging development, requiring a reorientation of thinking and methods. It does not, however, require a commitment to laissez-faire, balanced budgets, 4 percent growth rules, or to any substantive policy stance. Technical achievements have a remarkable history of following many masters.

Recent research into the financial market area has shown the power of a commitment to using the principle of rational expectations as a basis for guiding investigation. Its use has turned up puzzles and questions that may have gone unanalyzed without the maintained assumption that markets process information efficiently. The paradoxes encountered when information is distributed as a free good through the price system have spurred an impressive theoretical literature that may eventually provide a richer appreciation of the relative merits of centralized versus decentralized information processing and decision making.

Empirical work has turned up the need for further study of the determination of market risk premia if we wish to account for the behavior of security prices. The hypothesis that security prices are functions of conditional expectations has simply pushed the discussion one step further – why do the apparent risk premia exhibit so much variation over time? If changes in information about dividends cannot explain movements in stock prices, what can?

The rational expectations hypothesis has come a long way since the original articles by Muth. Our economic men now have beliefs consistent with their economic models. This is surely not the only plausible, reasonable, or even "rational" alternative. But it is an approach that has proved itself in the internal development of the profession and has and can be a common foundation for substantive research in many areas. Continued use of the hypothesis may be the best satisficing strategy.

BIBLIOGRAPHY

Abel, Andrew B. 1980. "Empirical Investment Equations: An Integrative Frame-work," in *On the State of Macro-Economics*, edited by K. Brunner and A. Meltzer. Carnegie-Rochester Conference Series on Public Policy, No. 12. Amsterdam: North Holland.

Alexander, Sidney S. 1964. "Price Movements in Speculative Markets: Trends or Random Walks," in *The Random Character of Stock Market Prices*, edited by Paul Cootner. Cambridge, Mass.: M.I.T. Press.

Allen, Beth. 1981. "Generic Existence of Completely Revealing Equilibria for Economies with Uncertainty When Prices Convey Information," *Econometrica* 49:1173–99.

Altonji, Joseph G. 1981. "The Intertemporal Substitution Model of Labor Market Fluctuations: An Empirical Analysis," Columbia University, Department of Economics Discussion Paper No. 107.

Askari, H., and Cummings, J. T. 1977. "Estimating Agricultural Supply Response with the Nerlove Model: A Survey," *International Economic Review* 18:257–92.

Azariadis, C. 1975. "Implicit Contracts and Unemployment Equilibria," *Journal of Political Economy* 83:1183–202.

1981. "A Reexamination of Natural Rate Theory," *American Economic Review* 71:946–60.

Bailey, M. N. 1974. "Wages and Employment Under Uncertain Demand," *Review of Economic Studies* 41:37–50.

Ball, Ray. 1978. "Anomalies in Relationships Between Securities' Yields and Yield-Surrogates," *Journal of Financial Economics* 6:103–26.

Barro, Robert J. 1977a. "Unanticipated Money Growth and Unemployment in the United States," *American Economic Review* 67:101–15.

1977b. "Long-term Contracting, Sticky Prices, and Monetary Policy," *Journal of Monetary Economics* 3:305–16.

1978. "Unanticipated Money, Output and the Price Level in the United States," *Journal of Political Economy* 86:549–80.

1979. "Unanticipated Money Growth and Unemployment in the United States: Reply," *American Economic Review* 69:1004–9.

1980a. "A Capital Market in an Equilibrium Business Cycle Model," *Econometrica* 48:1393–417.

1980b. "Federal Deficit Policy and the Effects of Public Debt Shocks," *Journal of Money, Credit, and Banking* 12:747–62.

Black, F. 1972. "Capital Market Equilibrium with Restricted Borrowing," *Journal of Business* July:444–55.

Black, F., M. C. Jensen, and M. Scholes. 1972. "The Capital Asset Pricing Model: Some Empirical Tests," in *Studies in the Theory of Capital Markets*, edited by M. C. Jensen. New York: Praeger.

Blanchard, Olivier J. 1979. "Wage Indexing Rules and the Behavior of the Economy," *Journal of Political Economy* 87:798–815.

1980. "The Monetary Mechanism in the Light of Rational Expectations," in *Rational Expectations and Economic Policy*, edited by Stanley Fischer. Chicago: National Bureau of Economic Research.

1981. "Output, the Stock Market, and Interest Rates," *American Economic Review* 71:132–43.

Blinder, Alan. 1979. *Economic Policy and the Great Stagflation*. New York: Academic Press.

Blinder, Alan S., and S. Fischer. 1981. "Inventories, Rational Expectations, and the Business Cycle," *Journal of Monetary Economics* 8:277–304.

Blume, Marshall. 1968. "The Assessment of Portfolio Performance." Unpublished Ph.D. thesis, University of Chicago.

Boschen, John F., and Herschel I. Grossman. 1980. "Tests of Equilibrium Macroeconomics Using Contemporaneous Monetary Data," NBER Working Paper 558.

Bray, Margaret. 1981. "Futures Trading, Rational Expectations, and the Efficient Markets Hypothesis," *Econometrica* 49:575–96.

Bray, Margaret, and David M. Kreps. 1981. "Rational Learning and Rational Expectations," Research Paper Series no. 616. Graduate School of Business, Stanford.

Brock, William A. 1975. "A Simple Perfect Foresight Monetary Model," *Journal of Monetary Economics* 1:133–50.

Buiter, Willem H. 1981. "Real Effects of Anticipated and Unanticipated Money: Some Problems of Estimation and Hypothesis Testing," NBER Working Paper no. 601.

Business Week. 1981. "The Experts Stick Pins in the Reagan Forecast," March 2.

Cagan, Phillip. 1956. "The Monetary Dynamics of Hyperinflation," in *Studies in the Quantity Theory of Money*, edited by Milton Friedman. Chicago: University of Chicago Press.

Calvo, Guillermo. 1978. "On the Time Consistency of Optimal Policy in a Monetary Economy," *Econometrica* 46:1411–28.

Carlson, John A. 1977. "A Study of Price Forecasts," *Annals of Economic and Social Measurement* 6:27–56.

Cootner, Paul (ed.). 1967. *The Random Character of Stock Market Prices*. Cambridge, Mass.: M.I.T. Press.

Cox, Charles C. 1976. "Futures Trading and Market Information," *Journal of Political Economy* 84:1215–36.

Cumby, R., Huizinga, J., and Obstfeld, M. 1981. "Two-Step Two-Stage Least Squares Estimation in Models with Rational Expectations," NBER Technical Paper No. 11.

Cyert, Richard M., and Morris H. DeGroot. 1974. "Rational Expectations and Bayesian Analysis," *Journal of Political Economy* 82:521–36.

DeCanio, Stephen J. 1979. "Rational Expectations and Learning from Experience," *Quarterly Journal of Economics* 370:47–57.

deLeeuw, F. D., and Ozanne L. 1981. "Housing," in *How Taxes Affect Economic Behavior*, edited by H. Aaron and J. Pechman. Washington, D.C.: The Brookings Institution.

Dornbusch, Rudiger. 1976. "Expectations and Exchange Rate Dynamics," *Journal of Political Economy* 84:1161–76.

Ezekiel, Morlecai. 1938. "The Cobweb Theorem," *Quarterly Journal of Economics* 52:255–80.

Fair, R. C. 1979. "An Analysis of a Macro-Economic Model with Rational Expectations in the Bond and Stock Markets," *American Economic Review* 69:539–52.

Fama, E. F. 1970. "Efficient Capital Markets: A Review of Theory and Empirical Work," *Journal of Finance* 25:383–423.

——— 1975. "Short-Term Interest Rates as Predictors of Inflation," *American Economic Review* 65:269–82.

——— 1976. *Foundations of Finance: Portfolio Decisions and Securities Prices*. New York: Basic Books.

Feldman, Mark. 1982. "Learning and Convergence to Rational Expectations," University of California, Santa Barbara, unpublished manuscript.

Feldstein, Martin. 1980. "Comments on 'A Competitive Theory of Fluctuations and the Feasibility and Desirability of Stabilization Policy,' " in *Rational Expectations and Economic Policy*, edited by Stanley Fischer. Chicago: National Bureau of Economic Research.

Fellner, William. 1979. "The Credibility Effect and Rational Expectations: Implications of the Gramlich Study," *Brookings Paper on Economic Activity* 1:167–78.

Figlewski, Stephen. 1980. "Optimal Price Forecasting Using Survey Data," New York University Graduate School of Business Administration.

Figlewski, S., and P. Wachtel. 1981. "The Formation of Inflationary Expectations," *Review of Economics and Statistics* 58:1–10.

Fischer, Stanley. 1977a. "Long-term Contracts, Rational Expectations, and the Optimal Money Supply Rule," *Journal of Political Economy* 85:191–205.

——— 1977b. "Long-term Contracting, Sticky Prices, and Monetary Policy: A Comment," *Journal of Monetary Economics* 3:317–23.

——— 1979. "Capital Accumulation on the Transition Path in a Monetary Optimizing Model," *Econometrica* 47:1433–9.

——— 1980. "Dynamic Inconsistency, Cooperation and the Benevolent Dissembling Government," *Journal of Economic Dynamics and Control* 2:93–107.

Freeman, Richard. 1971. *The Market for College-Trained Manpower; a Study in the Economics of Career Choice*. Cambridge, Mass.: Harvard University Press.

Frenkel, J. A. 1977. "The Forward Exchange Rate, Expectations, and the Demand for Money: The German Hyperinflation," *American Economic Review* 67:653–70.

Friedman, Benjamin. 1979. "Optimal Expectations and the Extreme Information Assumptions of 'Rational Expectations' Macromodels," *Journal of Monetary Economics* 5:23–41.

1980. "Survey Evidence on the 'Rationality' of Interest Rate Expectations," *Journal of Monetary Economics* 6:453–65.

Friedman, Milton. 1968. "The Role of Monetary Policy," *American Economic Review* 58:1–17.

Froyen, R. T., and R. N. Waud. 1980. "International Evidence on Output-Inflation Tradeoffs," *American Economic Review* 70:409–21.

Frydman, R. 1981. "Sluggish Price Adjustments and the Effectiveness of Monetary Policy Under Rational Expectations," *Journal of Money, Credit and Banking* 13:94–102.

Gibson, William E. 1972. "Interest Rates and Inflationary Expectations: New Evidence," *American Economic Review* 62:854–65.

Goodwin, Thomas, and Sheffrin, Steven M. 1982. "Testing the Rational Expectations Hypothesis in an Agricultural Market," forthcoming, *Review of Economics and Statistics*.

Gordon, Robert J. 1981. "Price Inertia and Policy Ineffectiveness in the United States, 1890–1980," Northwestern University and NBER.

Grossman, Jacob. 1979. "Nominal Demand Policy and Short-Run Fluctuations in Unemployment and Prices in the United States," *Journal of Political Economy* 87:1063–85.

Grossman, Sanford. 1976. "On the Efficiency of Competitive Stock Markets Where Traders Have Diverse Information," *Journal of Finance* 31:573–85.

1978. "Further Results on the Informational Efficiency of Competitive Stock Markets," *Journal of Economic Theory* 18:81–101.

Grossman, S., and R. Shiller. 1981. "The Determinants of the Variability of Stock Prices," *American Economic Review* 71:222–7.

Grossman, Sanford J., and Joseph E. Stiglitz. 1976. "Information and Competitive Price Systems," *American Economic Review* 66:246–53.

1980. "The Impossibility of Informationally Efficient Markets," *American Economic Review* 70:393–408.

Hall, Robert E. 1976. "The Phillips Curve and Macroeconomic Policy," in *The Phillips Curves and Labor Markets*, edited by Karl Brunner and Allan H. Meltzer. Carnegie-Rochester Conference Series on Public Policy No. 1. Amsterdam: North Holland.

1978. "Stochastic Implications of the Life Cycle-Permanent Income Hypothesis: Theory and Evidence," *Journal of Political Economy* 86:971–87.

1980. "Labor Supply and Aggregate Fluctuations," in *On the State of Macro-Economics*, edited by K. Brunner and A. Meltzer. Carnegie-Rochester Conference Series on Public Policy No. 12. Amsterdam: North Holland.

Hall, Robert E., and David M. Lilien. 1979. "Efficient Wage Bargains Under Uncertain Supply and Demand," *American Economic Review* 69:868–79.

Hansen, Lars Peter, and Robert J. Hodrick. 1980. ''Forward Exchange Rates as Optimal Predictors of Future Spot Rates: An Econometric Analysis,'' *Journal of Political Economy* 88:829–53.

Hansen, L. P., and T. J. Sargent. 1980. ''Formulating and Estimating Dynamic Linear Rational Expectations Models,'' *Journal of Economic Dynamics and Control* 1:7–46.

Hayek, F. A. 1945. ''The Use of Knowledge in Society,'' *American Economic Review* 35:519–30.

Hirsch, Albert, and Michael C. Lowell. 1969. *Sales Anticipations and Inventory Behavior*. New York: Wiley.

Holt, Charles C., Franco Modigliani, John F. Muth, and Herbert A. Simon. 1960. *Planning Production, Inventories and Work Force*. Englewood Cliffs, N.J.: Prentice-Hall.

Huntzinger, R. L. 1979. ''Market Analysis with Rational Expectations,'' *Journal of Econometrics* 10:127–45.

Irvine, R. Owen, Jr. 1981. ''Tests of the Rationality and Accuracy of Manufacturers' Sales Expectations.'' Working Paper Series, National Income Section Wages, Prices, and Productivity Section, Board of Governors Federal Reserve System.

Jensen, Michael. 1978. ''Some Anomalous Evidence Regarding Market Efficiency,'' *Journal of Financial Economics* 6:95–101.

———. 1979. ''Tests of Capital Market Theory and Implications of the Evidence,'' in *Handbook of Financial Economics*, edited by James L. Bicksler. Amsterdam: North Holland.

Kantor, Brian. 1979. ''Rational Expectations and Economic Thought,'' *Journal of Economic Literature* 17:1422–41.

Kearl, James. 1979. ''Inflation, Mortgages, Housing,'' *Journal of Political Economy* 87:1115–38.

Kendall, Maurice G. 1953. ''The Analysis of Economic Time-Series, Part I: Prices,'' *Journal of the Royal Statistical Society* 96:11–25.

Keynes, J. M. 1964. *The General Theory of Employment, Interest, and Money*. New York: Harcourt, Brace and World.

King, Robert G. 1981. ''Monetary Information and Monetary Neutrality,'' *Journal of Monetary Economics* 7:195–206.

Kuhn, Thomas S. 1970. *The Structure of Scientific Revolutions*, 2d ed. Chicago: University of Chicago Press.

Kydland, Finn E., and Edward C. Prescott. 1977. ''Rules Rather than Discretion: The Inconsistency of Optimal Plans,'' *Journal of Political Economy* 85:473–91.

———. 1980. ''A Competitive Theory of Fluctuations and the Feasibility and Desirability of Stabilization Policy,'' in *Rational Expectations and Economic Policy*, edited by Stanley Fischer. Chicago: National Bureau of Economic Research.

Leiderman, Leonardo. 1980. ''Macroeconometric Testing of the Rational Expectations and Structural Neutrality Hypotheses for the United States,'' *Journal of Monetary Economics* 6:69–82.

LeRoy, Stephen F. 1973. ''Risk Aversion and the Martingale Property of Stock Prices,'' *International Economic Review* 14:436–46.

LeRoy, Stephen F. and Richard D. Porter. 1981. "The Present-Value Relation: Tests Based on Implied Variance Bounds," *Econometrica* 49:555–74.

Lintner, John. 1965. "The Valuation of Risk Assets and the Selection of Risky Investments in Stock Portfolios and Capital Budgets," *Review of Economics and Statistics* 47:13–37.

Lipsey, Richard G. 1960. "The Relation Between Unemployment and the Rate of Money Wage Changes in the United Kingdom, 1862–1957: A Further Analysis," *Economica* 27:1–31.

Lovell, M. 1976. "Inventory Behavior in Durable-Goods Manufacturing: The Target-Adjustment Model," in *Brookings Paper in Economic Activity: 2*, edited by Arthur Okun and George L. Perry. Washington, D.C.: The Brookings Institution.

Lucas, Robert E., Jr. 1972. "Expectations and the Neutrality of Money," *Journal of Economic Theory* 4:103–24.

  1973. "Some International Evidence on Output-Inflation Trade-offs," *American Economic Review* 63:326–34.

  1975. "An Equilibrium Model of the Business Cycle," *Journal of Political Economy* 83:1113–44.

  1976. "Econometric Policy Evaluation: A Critique," in *The Phillips Curve and Labor Markets*, edited by Karl Brunner and Allan H. Meltzer. Amsterdam: North Holland.

  1977. "Understanding Business Cycles," in *Stabilization of the Domestic and International Economy*, edited by Karl Brunner and Allan Meltzer. Carnegie-Rochester Conference Series in Public Policy. Amsterdam: North Holland.

  1978a. "Asset Prices in an Exchange Economy," *Econometrica* 46:1429–45.

  1978b. "Unemployment Policy," *American Economic Review* 68:353–7.

  1980a. "Methods and Problems in Business Cycle Theory," *Journal of Money Credit and Banking* 12:696–715.

  1980b. "Rules, Discretion, and the Role of the Economic Advisor," in *Rational Expectations and Economic Policy*, edited by Stanley Fischer. Chicago: National Bureau of Economic Research.

Lucas, R. E., Jr., and Rapping, L. A. 1970. "Real Wages, Employment and Inflation," in E. S. Phelps (ed.), *Microeconomic Foundations of Employment and Inflation Theory*. New York: Norton.

Lucas, R. E., Jr., and Sargent, T. J. 1978. "After Keynesian Macroeconomics," in *After the Phillips Curve: Persistence of High Inflation and High Unemployment*. Federal Reserve Bank of Boston Conference, Vol. 19, Boston: Federal Reserve Bank, pp. 49–72.

McCallum, Bennett T. 1976. "Rational Expectations and the Natural Rate Hypothesis: Some Consistent Estimates," *Econometrica* 44:43–52.

  1977. "Price-Level Stickiness and the Feasibility of Monetary Stabilization Policy with Rational Expectations," *Journal of Political Economy* 85:627–34.

  1979. "On the Observational Equivalence of Classical and Keynesian Models," *Journal of Political Economy* 87:395–402.

  1980. "Rational Expectations and Macroeconomic Stabilization Policy," *Journal of Money, Credit, and Banking* 12:716–46.

Mayer, Thomas. 1978. *The Structure of Monetarism*. New York: Norton.

Meltzer, Allan. 1978. "Monetarist, Keynesian and Quantity Theories," in *The Structure of Monetarism*, edited by Thomas Mayer. New York: Norton.

Mishkin, Frederic S. 1978. "Efficient-Markets Theory: Implications for Monetary Policy," in *Brookings Paper on Economic Activity*, edited by A. Okun and G. L. Perry. Vol. 3, pp. 707–68.

―― 1979. "Simulation Methodology in Macroeconomics: An Innovation Technique," *Journal of Political Economy* 87:816–36.

―― 1981a. "Monetary Policy and Long-term Interest Rates: An Efficient Markets Approach," *Journal of Monetary Economics* 7:29–55.

―― 1981b. "Are Market Forecasts Rational?" *American Economic Review* 71:293–306.

―― 1981c. "The Real Interest Rate: An Empirical Investigation," in *Carnegie Rochester Conference Series on Public Policy: The Costs and Consequences of Inflation*, edited by Karl Brunner and Allan H. Meltzer. Vol. 15, pp. 151–200.

―― 1982. "Does Anticipated Monetary Policy Matter? An Econometric Investigation," *Journal of Political Economy* 90:22–51.

Modigliani, Franco. 1977. "The Monetarists Controversy or, Should We Forsake Stabilization Policies?" *American Economic Review* 67:1–19.

Mossin, J. 1966. "Equilibrium in a Capital Asset Market," *Econometrica* 34:768–83.

Mullineaux, Donald J. 1978. "On Testing for Rationality: Another Look at the Livingston Price Expectations Data," *Journal of Political Economy* 86:329–36.

Muth, John F. 1960. "Optimal Properties of Exponentially Weighted Forecasts," *Journal of the American Statistical Association* 55:299–306.

―― 1961. "Rational Expectations and the Theory of Price Movements," *Econometrica* 29:315–35.

Nelson, Charles R. 1975. "Rational Expectations and the Predictive Efficiency of Economic Models," *Journal of Business* 48:331–43.

Nelson, C. R., and G. W. Schwert. 1977. "On Testing the Hypothesis That the Real Rate of Interest Is Constant," *American Economic Review* 67:478–86.

Nerlove, Marc. 1958. "Adaptive Expectations and Cobweb Phenomena," *Quarterly Journal of Economics* 73:227–40.

Nordhaus, William D. 1976. "Comments on 'Contract Theory and the Moderation of Inflation by Recession and by Controls'." *Brookings Papers on Economic Activity*, pp. 623–7.

Oakeshott, Michael. 1962. *Rationalism in Politics*. New York: Basic Books.

Okun, Arthur M. 1981. *Prices and Quantities*. Washington D.C.: The Brookings Institution.

Patinkin, Don. 1965. *Money, Interest, and Prices; An Integration of Monetary and Value Theory*, 2d ed. New York: Harper & Row.

Pauls, B. Dianne. 1979. "The Relation Between Market-Specific and Aggregate Price Forecast Errors: A Test of the Partial Information Assumption," unpublished manuscript, M.I.T.

Pearce, Douglas K. 1979. "Comparing Survey and Rational Measures of Expected Inflation," *Journal of Money, Credit, and Banking* 11:447–56.

Peck, Anne E. 1976. "Future Markets, Supply Response, and Price Stability," *Quarterly Journal of Economics* 90:407–23.

Perry, George L. 1966. *Unemployment, Money Wage Rates, and Inflation*, Cambridge. Mass.: M.I.T. Press.

Pesando, James E. 1975. "A Note on the Rationality of the Livingston Price Expectations," *Journal of Political Economy* 83:849–58.

Phelps, Edmund S. 1970. "The New Microeconomics in Employment and Inflation Theory," in *Microeconomic Foundations of Employment and Inflation Theory*, edited by Phelps. New York: Norton.

1972. *Inflation Policy and Unemployment Theory: The Cost-Benefit Approach to Monetary Planning*. New York: Norton.

Phelps, Edmund S., and John B. Taylor. 1977. "Stabilizing Properties of Monetary Policy Under Rational Expectations," *Journal of Political Economy* 84:163–90.

Phillips, A. W. 1958. "The Relation Between Unemployment and the Rate of Change of Money Wage Rates in the United Kingdom, 1861–1957," *Economica* 25:283–94.

Poole, William. 1976. "Rational Expectations in the Macro Model," in *Brookings Papers on Economic Activity*, edited by A. Okun and G. Perry. Vol. 2: pp. 463–514.

Poterba, James M. 1980. "Inflation, Income Taxes, and Owner Occupied Housing." National Bureau of Economic Research Working Paper No. 553.

Prescott, Edward C. 1977. "Should Control Theory Be Used for Economic Stabilization?" in *Optimal Policies, Control Theory and Technology Exports*, edited by Karl Brunner and Alan H. Meltzer. Carnegie-Rochester Conference Series on Public Policy. Amsterdam: North Holland.

Radner, Roy. 1979. "Rational Expectations Equilibrium: Generic Existence and the Information Revealed by Prices," *Econometrica* 47:655–78.

Ramsey, Frank P. 1927. "A Contribution to the Theory of Taxation," *Economic Journal* 37:47–61.

Rappoport, P. 1980. "Rational Expectations and Rationality," unpublished paper. Berkeley: University of California, Department of Economics.

Roll, Richard. 1977. "A Critique of the Asset Pricing Theory's Tests; Part I: On Past and Potential Testability of the Theory," *Journal of Financial Economics* 4:129–76.

Rowen, Hobart. 1981. "Economic U-Turn," *Washington Post*, February 12.

Samuelson, Paul A. 1965. *Foundations of Economic Analysis*. New York: Atheneum.

1972. "Proof That Properly Anticipated Prices Fluctuate Randomly," in *The Collected Scientific Papers of Paul A. Samuelson*, edited by Robert Merton. Vol. 3. Cambridge, Mass.: M.I.T. Press.

Sargent, Thomas J. 1976. "The Observational Equivalence of Natural and Unnatural Rate Theories of Macroeconomics," *Journal of Political Economy* 84:631–40.

1978. "Estimation of Dynamic Labor Demand Schedules Under Rational Expectations," *Journal of Political Economy* 86:1009–44.

1979. *Macroeconomic Theory*. New York: Academic Press.

1981a. "Interpreting Economic Time Series," *Journal of Political Economy* 89:213–48.

1981b. "The Ends of Four Big Inflations," National Bureau of Economic Research, Conference Paper No. 90.

Sargent, Thomas J., and Neil Wallace. 1975. "Rational Expectations, the Optimal Monetary Instrument and the Optimal Money Supply Rule," *Journal of Political Economy* 83:241–54.

1976. "Rational Expectations and the Theory of Economic Policy," *Journal of Monetary Economics* 2:169–84.

Savage, L. J. 1954. *The Foundations of Statistics*. New York: Wiley.

Sharpe, William F. 1964. "Capital Asset Prices: A Theory of Market Equilibrium Under Conditions of Risk," *Journal of Finance* 19:425–42.

Sheffrin, Steven M. 1979. "Unanticipated Money Growth and Output Fluctuations," *Economic Inquiry* 17:1–13.

Shiller, Robert J. 1978. "Rational Expectations and the Dynamic Structure of Macroeconomic Models," *Journal of Monetary Economics* 4:1–44.

1980. "Can the Fed Control Real Interest Rates?" in *Rational Expectations and Economic Policy*, edited by Stanley Fisher. Chicago: The University of Chicago Press.

1981a. "Do Stock Prices Move Too Much to Be Justified by Subsequent Changes in Dividends?" *American Economic Review* 71:421–36.

1981b. "The Use of Volatility Measures in Assessing Market Efficiency," *Journal of Finance* 36:291–304.

1982. "Consumption, Asset Markets, and Macroeconomic Fluctuations," National Bureau of Economic Research Working Paper No. 838.

Sidrauski, M. 1967. "Rational Choice and Patterns of Growth in a Monetary Economy," *American Economic Review* 57:534–44.

Simon, Herbert A. 1956. "Dynamic Programming Under Uncertainty with a Quadratic Criterion Function," *Econometrica* 24:74–81.

1979. "Rational Decision Making in Business Organizations," *American Economic Review* 64:493–513.

Simons, Henry C. 1936. "Rules Versus Authorities in Monetary Policy," *Journal of Political Economy* 44:1–30.

Sims, Christopher A. 1980. "Macroeconomics and Reality," *Econometrica* 48:1–48.

Small, David H. 1979. "Unanticipated Money Growth and Unemployment in the United States: Comment," *American Economic Review* 69:996–1003.

Solow, Robert M. 1980. "On Theories of Unemployment," *American Economic Review* 70:1–11.

Swamy, P. A. V. B., Barth, J. R., and Tinsley, P. A., 1982. "The Rational Expectations Approach to Economic Modelling," *Journal of Economic Dynamics and Control* 4:125–48.

Taylor, John B. 1977. "Conditions for Unique Solutions in Stochastic Macroeconomic Models with Rational Expectations," *Econometrica* 45:1377–85.

1979. "Estimation and Control of a Macroeconomic Model with Rational Expectations," *Econometrica* 47:1267–86.

1980. "Aggregate Dynamics and Staggered Contracts," *Journal of Political Economy* 88:1–23.

1981. "Stabilization, Accommodation, and Monetary Rules," *American Economic Review Papers and Proceedings* 71:145–9.

Tobin, James. 1965. "Money and Economic Growth," *Econometrica* 33:671–84.

1977. "How Dead Is Keynes?" *Economic Inquiry* 15:459–68.

1981. "The Monetarist Counter-Revolution Today – An Appraisal," *Economic Journal* 91:29–42.

Turnovsky, Stephen J. 1970. "Some Empirical Evidence on the Formation of Price Expectations," *Journal of the American Statistical Association* 65:1441–54.

1979. "Futures Markets, Private Storage, and Price Stabilization," *Journal of Public Economics* 12:301–27.

Tversky, Amos, and Kahneman, Daniel. 1974. "Judgment Under Uncertainty: Heuristics and Biases," *Science* 185:1124–31.

Wallis, Kenneth F. 1980. "Econometric Implications of the Rational Expectations Hypothesis," *Econometrica* 48:49–73.

Watts, Ross L. 1978. "Systemic 'Abnormal' Returns After Quarterly Earnings Announcements," *Journal of Financial Economics* 6:127–50.

Weiss, Laurence. 1980. "The Role for Active Monetary Policy in a Rational Expectations Model," *Journal of Political Economy* 2:221–33.

Witte, James. 1963. "The Microfoundations of the Social Investment Function," *Journal of Political Economy* 71:441–56.

INDEX